People Succession
Lessons from Forward Thinking Executives in Middle-Market Companies

by Carol Bergeron

Talent Magnet Series™
Burlington, Massachusetts

Published by: Talent Magnet Series™, Burlington, Massachusetts

Printed in the United States of America

ISBN: 978-0-9887071-0-8

LCCN: 2012955011

This publication is designed to provide accurate information in
regard to the subject matter covered though the strategies contained
herein may not be suitable for your situation. It is sold with the
understanding that neither the author nor the publisher is engaged in
rendering legal, accounting, securities trading, or other professional
services. If legal advice or other expert assistance is required, the
services of a competent professional person should be sought.

For information about special discounts for bulk purchases, please
contact the author:
www.bergeronassociates.com/content/contact-us

Table of Contents

Forethought

During the normal course of running my business, it is commonplace for me to converse with executives in middle-market companies regarding their organizations' achievements, vision, aspirations, and big lofty goals for the future. It's nearly impossible not to get caught up in the whirlwind of pride, enthusiasm, and optimism they have for the organizations they lead. And that's saying a lot, especially after having survived the most severe economic downturn experienced in the United States in nearly 80 years.

After inquiring and understanding more about the factors that will move their organizations forward it's not long before the conversations shift. Obstacles, impediments, and challenges of both the external and internal variety that could derail their best intentions are revealed. And invariably one of the top three challenges nearly all the executives lose sleep over includes workforce issues such as:

- Do we have the right mix of talent to achieve our goals?

- Is the talent mix robust enough to overcome the obstacles we know of today? How about the unknown challenges of tomorrow?

- What business performance will suffer or business opportunities will be missed if mission critical positions are not filled quickly enough or are filled with people not fully prepared?

- How proficient are we at filling key positions that open unexpectedly or expectedly?

- Shifting workforce demographics are already creating havoc with the ability to attract and retain top talent. How do we more proactively, creatively, and effectively deal with this challenge?

As optimistic as the executives are about the future, you cannot mistake the anxiety and even frustration in their voices as they speak of talent challenges. Naturally, the conversations shift direction yet again to potential talent solutions with keen interest in those that worked well at other middle-market companies.

It was these commonplace conversations that prompted me to sit down and write this book. Why? Because there are middle-market and aspiring middle-market executives who have struggled with the same challenges, asked the same questions, sought out solutions, and successfully made succession planning and management (SPM) work at their organizations. My purpose in writing this book is to facilitate peer learning, in print, among executives in middle-market companies. The organizations I work with know of the many benefits effective talent management solutions like SPM provide. Spreading the word in print, however, allows the solutions to reach a much larger audience that cannot be achieved by working with one individual company after another. Think of this publication as peer learning in print to benefit a broader audience.

Consider some high visibility SPM events:

General Electric – Jack F. Welch Jr. announces his retirement after 20 years at the helm. He selects Jeffrey R. Immelt, then an 18-year veteran of GE and one of three internal candidates, as his successor effective September 2001. Immelt continues to lead the global organization some 12 years later.

IBM – Samuel J. Palmisano, after 12 years serving as President and another 27 years serving in sales and general management roles at Big Blue, passes the baton in 2012 to Ginni Rometty, a 31-year veteran of IBM.

You're probably wondering how these examples could be relevant to middle-market and aspiring middle-market company executives. Simple: Because all these companies were middle-market companies earlier in their organizational development.

No doubt the leaders of these now large global firms and others like them encountered their fair share of business disruptions due to one talent debacle followed by another. At what point did these leaders stop and think about how to cease the talent disruptions? At what point did they realize that the unrelenting demographic shifts in the workforce weren't going away and would in fact get worse? At what point did they decide that "enough is enough!" and choose to step up their game with talent solutions that put them in the driver's seat?

I suspect that "ah-ha" moment came about after dealing with a series of staffing crises topped off by a whopper: a job vacancy that significantly impacted business operations and performance took a hit as a result; disappointment so unforgettable that it left an indelible mark on their psyche; a hardship so momentous that they chose to stop the madness by taking ownership for talent issues over which they do influence!

The biggest difference between you, an executive in a middle-market company, and them, C-level executives in large organizations, may simply be that they already chose to build an internal talent pool as a key source of candidates to satisfy future talent needs. Why? First and foremost, because it reduces the risk of disruptions in business operations and performance. Second, skilled, talented people are a differentiator in pulling off big lofty growth goals.

This book captures lessons learned by executives in middle-market companies who have taken ownership for building an internal talent pool at their respective organizations. I interviewed over 25 executives over a six-month period either on the phone or in person at the executives' offices, coffee shops, restaurants, and even a library. Why did it take six months? First, scheduling time with executives can be challenging given their travel and meeting schedules. Second, because nearly all of the first 15 interviews were with men who provided wonderful insight. I could not help but feel that women needed strong representation. So, I reached out to my network for help identifying women executives who'd be willing to participate. They did not disappoint.

Interviews lasted an hour or two each. I asked questions regarding their first-hand experiences with SPM. Some executives' lessons stemmed from their experiences in developing people for future responsibilities. Others reminisced about their own career progression over the years and their key takeaways. All their feedback provided a basis for profound learning. I am confident that the executives were telling me the truth because emotions came flooding back as they shared their experiences, strong emotions as if the experiences happened just yesterday. Plus, their forthrightness was evident and their detailed level of recall remarkable.

With few exceptions, nearly all the executives interviewed lead organizations with revenue in the range of $30M to $1B. Some organizations are family-owned, some are venture or private equity-backed, a few are publicly traded, a few are entities (i.e. a division, subsidiary, joint venture) within large global firms, and a state agency. Some executives have permitted me to disclose their real names, companies, and/or titles; others requested anonymity. When introducing you to them throughout the book I honor their preferences.

The main themes among the executives interviewed include:

- An unwavering desire to position their organizations for growth and to manage risk, all major risks, that could compromise that growth.

And managing risk includes establishing the right balance of short and long-term talent solutions in support of business goal achievement. Makes sense given human capital is often the biggest investment companies make, one of the most dynamic of all resources managed, and the most powerful lever in organizational performance.

- A deep-seeded belief that proactive management of talent is their duty despite competing demands for their time. They choose to make people and talent management a priority with or without the formality of talent management or SPM processes.

- The recognition that future skill and talent shortages, the complexities of managing a multigenerational workforce, changing workforce demographics, flatter organizations, the acceleration of technological advancements, and the global marketplace are macro factors that aren't going away anytime soon. Though they have no control over the macro factors and trends, they choose to proactively address those things over which they do have influence.

- They promote a talent management journey where solutions are practical, adaptable, sustainable, and tightly linked to business strategy. They do not fall victim to one-time talent interventions. They dismiss the notions that talent solutions are dispensable in tough economic times or that they have to break the bank in order to be effective.

- Personally, the executives get a kick out of helping others succeed. Having contributed to people growing more confident in their abilities, taking on more responsibility and advancing their careers is very rewarding. Some of the executives were inspired by great role models who aided them in their own growth, while others just want to make it a little easier for the next person to succeed. And hands down, proactively preparing people for future success is much more fun than its corrective action alternatives: managing performance problems, terminations, re-organizations, or worse, putting organizational growth plans on hold due to the absence of critical skills and talent.

My first objective is that by the time you finish reading this book you can imagine what it would be like to have many more options when it comes to assembling and redeploying a robust, adaptable, and high performing workforce. My second objective is that you will make SPM a priority and enlist others in your organization to build an internal talent pool as a risk management imperative. Think of SPM as an insurance policy for one of the largest investments made at your organization – human capital.

Envision the day when the vice president of sales retires earlier than planned. You're not worried, and neither is anyone else on the executive leadership team. Why not? Because you have been grooming his successor and he's ready. How about when your organization wins a new contract tripling the number of mammoth sized cross-functional projects (and the revenue too)? It doesn't faze you because over the last two years you have built a cadre of project managers and team players, all of whom proficiently use a common set of flexible project management tools and get results. The regional manager in Europe flees to a warmer climate. So, you send an employee, in training for a business unit manager role, on an expatriate assignment for several years in the role of country manager. The chief financial officer unexpectedly goes out on long-term disability. Not to worry since the controller steps into the role. And when your chief scientist gets wooed to join the competition, she passes the baton to her second in command. The scientist's successor had a development plan that included authoring and presenting papers at umpteen industry conferences which helps preserve company brand in the marketplace too.

Those are the kind of experiences executives in middle-market companies can realize when committing to SPM. Will things work out perfectly every time? No, not given the array of moving parts when it comes to talent. Though having ready-to-go options when it comes to redeploy people is an objective of SPM. And those options can produce not only a domino effect in terms of career growth opportunities for a number of employees; they also lead to some level of peace of mind among executives so that they can lose sleep over other things.

Just a few remarks on how this book is organized. The first chapter focuses on the business case and drivers for SPM. The next chapter is an overview of the seven steps in a formal SPM process so you get a good sense for what's involved and the importance of each step. And like any talent solution, SPM should support achievement of organizational goals. Chapter 3, The School of Hard Knocks, captures a few unforgettable first-hand business experiences that prompted the executives to make SPM a priority throughout their careers. In Chapter 4, Career Champions, several executives share their personal experiences of career advancement and their most significant lessons that deliberately get passed onto others. Chapter 5, Climate Counts, reinforces the importance of implementing SPM in a climate conducive to learning so that inspiring growth can be as easy as the "1 - 2 - 3 Debrief." The next couple of chapters, Derail the Derailers and Derailer 9: Career Conversations, run through the most frequently encountered derailers to SPM implementation, as well as true experiences and how to deal with the derailers; after all, forewarned is forearmed. At the heart of SPM is preparing people for future responsibilities. Chapter 8, The Talent Magnet Tool Kit, walks through a menu of development approaches from which executives select depending on goals, resources, and employee learning styles. It is loaded with examples shared by the executives interviewed. Chapter 9, Wanted: Blue Boxers, speaks to the very tightly woven interdependencies between grooming a pipeline of internal candidates through SPM and hiring external candidates. Insights and nuances associated with SPM responsibilities of the board of directors are discussed as are talent analytics used to measure progress of SPM in Chapter 10. In Chapter 11, Ready, Set, Go, executive decision making involving the redeployment of people is addressed. In Afterthoughts, we simply wrap up.

People Succession

Acknowledgements

Writing a book has been on my bucket list for some time. My passion for helping organizations and people soar inspired me throughout the entire writing process. This undertaking, however, could not have been possible without help from a host of people.

Many thanks to the forward thinking middle-market executives who graciously agreed to participate in interviews. Their generous spirit and first-hand accounts of pivotal experiences reflect their fundamental belief to pass onto others the lessons they have learned thus far on their own leadership journeys. You will be introduced to these executives throughout the book.

In an effort to expand my reach beyond my clients and to a broader range of companies and industries, there were a number of folks who went out of their way to introduce me to executives who had stories to tell. Many thanks to Leslie Ackles, Doug Cox, Hank Flores, Jean Johnson, Ben Procter, Katherine Rogers, Vanessa Schaefer, and Paul Tessier.

Dave Bergeron, Steve Bergeron, Joanne Lehner, and Jane Tessier, thank you for being so enthusiastic and supportive in addition to taking the time to read my manuscript and provide valuable feedback when needed most.

To Ken Lizotte, Elena Petricone and Lauren Fleming, my editors, many thanks for guiding me through the scoping, book writing, publishing and printing maze. It has been quite a learning experience. To Cindy Murphy, thank you for your expertise and persistence on all layout matters. To Thomas Bergeron, many thanks for your creativity on the book cover design.

All of you were instrumental in making this publication a reality. Many thanks.

Chapter 1

Why Succession Planning and Management Matters

Why does succession planning & management (SPM) matter? Because as a key component to a talent strategy (Figure 1-1) SPM operates as a catalyst for creating competitive advantage and improved organizational performance including revenue, profits, productivity, customer satisfaction, quality, and market capitalization. And when executed well, attracting, developing, engaging, deploying, and retaining top talent gets easier. Please allow me to elaborate starting with macro level labor trends.

Figure 1-1: Elements of a Talent Strategy

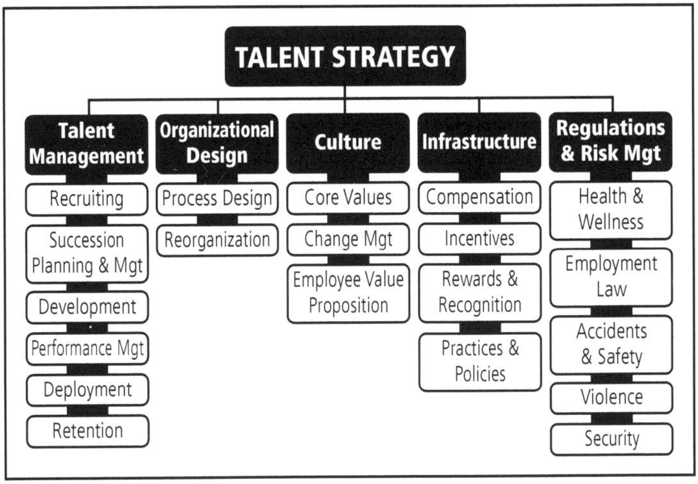

The talent strategy, an output of strategic workforce planning, describes: the nature of work to be done by the organization, the people and mission critical capabilities needed now and in the future to perform that work, the availability of talent, and an action plan to address short and long-term shortages and surpluses of people and capabilities. The talent strategy includes five broad clusters: talent management, organizational design, culture, infrastructure, and regulations and risk management. SPM is a key component in the talent management cluster.

Shortages in Skills and Availability of Top Talent

There are data points important to recognize in the talent equation. They include the macro level external factors resulting in shortages in skills and availability of talent. Factors include:

- The aging population (Figure 1-2) – The drop off in population from Baby Boomers to Generation X is contributing to talent shortages.

- Generational workforce issues – Employers must get creative in attracting, engaging, and retaining employees in all generations; this will require far more flexible people practices and workforce arrangements than ever before.

- Greater ethnic diversity – Employers who proactively embrace a more diverse workforce will benefit greatly from a broader range of thinking and perspectives.

- More women in the workforce and the changing family structure.

- Deficits in science, technology, engineering and mathematics graduates and workers.

- Domestic and global economic volatility.

- Technological advancements – Technology changes the way work gets done thus increasing the training and educational needs of the workforce.

Figure 1-2: 2010 US Population

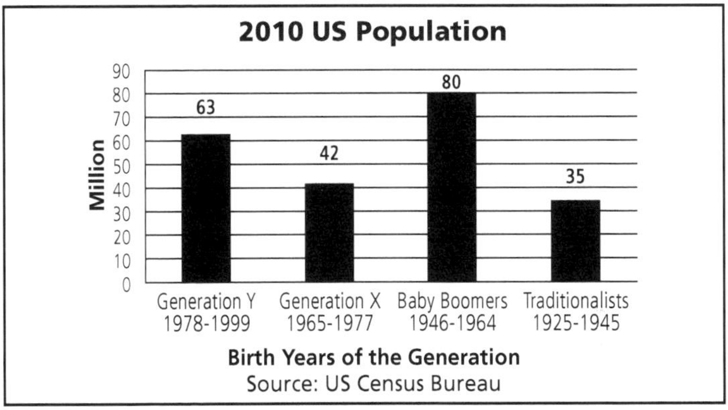

2010 US Population

Source: US Census Bureau

Top Performing Companies Take On the Uncontrollables

An *Enterprise Performance Management Study*[1] conducted by Bergeron Associates™ and Insight Management Group revealed that "external factors" was cited by top performing organizations as one of the top three impediments to meeting organizational performance expectations. The study explained that top performing organizations were astute in recognizing and addressing factors they can control such as poor execution, competing priorities, and unrealistic expectations. The executives of these organizations were quick to point out that factors over which they have little or no control (the economy, business cycles, macro level labor trends and the like) have to be effectively dealt with as well. Thus, they take steps to anticipate, recognize, and deal with the uncontrollables sooner rather than later.

Companies Leave Money on the Table

A recent study completed by the AICPA and CIMA[2] reported that deficiencies in human capital management are preventing organizations from: achieving operational and financial targets, successfully pursuing business growth opportunities, and innovating at a time when innovation is a game changer. The deficiencies are largely attributable to inadequate talent analytics to support decision making, failure to embed talent management into the business strategy and insufficient means to measure the returns on talent management investments.

A study conducted by The Boston Consulting Group[3] revealed that companies proficient or "highly skilled" in core human capital management practices achieve as much as 3.5 times the revenue growth and up to 2 times the profit margins of companies less capable in the same human capital practices.

These are but two of many studies that make the same point. Insufficient talent management hurts the top and bottom lines of businesses across industries. It pays to get good at talent management.

Employees Demand Career Growth

Blessing White's *Employee Engagement Report 2011*[4] found in North America:

- Only about one third of workers are engaged.

- Top engagement drivers include "more opportunity to do what I do best" (27%) closely followed by "career development opportunities and training" (20%).

- Among the engaged workers 81% "definitely intend to stay with their employers" compared with only 18% among the disengaged.

- "Lack of career opportunities" (28%) was cited by engaged and unengaged workers as the top reason for considering leaving current employer.

Right Management's *Employee Engagement - Maximizing Organizational Performance*[5] study indicates that employee engagement is very strongly linked to customer satisfaction, employee retention and financial performance. The study found that only 1/3 of employees are engaged. The study reported that highly engaged work groups scored higher: 44% higher in retention, 50% more productive, 33% more profitable and 56% higher in customer loyalty. Imagine the organizational performance improvements possible if all employees were engaged.

When addressing talent management issues that support business goal achievement, do not underestimate the impact the loss of mission critical capabilities will have on the long-term economic outlook of organizations. Let me explain.

Economic Impact due to Key Executive Departure

Vastly underestimating the economic impact of a key employee departure happens far too often. Typically only one-time costs associated with replacement hiring are considered. The estimates commonly include costs attributable to: the time of internal personnel spent on recruiting, the search fee, new hire sign on bonus, net increase in salary of the new hire, new hire acclimation and administrative costs, temporary help, and productivity losses due to the job vacancy. They may also include relocation and so forth. Let me walk you through the potential economic impact organizations face when a key employee departs.

Imagine that you are the president of a five-million dollar high-technology company. Your executive team pulled together a simple five-year business model (Table 1-1) based on decisions made in strategic planning sessions which reflects the following assumptions:

- Current product revenue is $5M and is expected to grow 10% annually.

- 1st new product launch is planned for July in year 2 and is expected to generate $2M in sales annually with a 15% annual growth rate.

- 2nd new product launch is planned for April in year 3 and is expected to generate $1M in sales annually with a 10% annual growth rate.

- 3rd new product launch is planned for January in year 4 and is expected to generate $4M in sales annually with a 10% annual growth rate.

- Cost of goods sold is 35% of sales.

- Research and development (R&D) expense is expected to be 15% of sales; no non-recurring R&D expense.

- Sales, general, and administrative costs are expected to be 12% of sales.

- Chief technology officer (CTO) base salary is $200k with bonus and benefit run rate at 25% and 30% of base salary respectively.

There are a few things to know about the three business model tables that follow. First, sales from current and three new products are itemized so that revenue levels attributable to the timing of new product launches is evident over a five-year period. Second, both recurring and non-recurring R&D expenses are itemized so that costs attributable to the unexpected departure of a key employee are unmistakable. Third, definitions used:

COGs = cost of goods sold

SG&A = sales, general, and administrative costs

EBITDA = gross revenue less expenses excluding tax, interest, depreciation & amortization; an indicator of the company's financial performance.

Your company is expected to increase its annual revenue from $5M in year 1 to nearly $16M in year 5; $50M in sales cumulatively over the five years.

Table 1-1: Planned Business Performance (in thousands)

	Year 1	Year 2	Year 3	Year 4	Year 5
Sales Current Products @ 10% growth	$5,000	$5,500	$6,050	$6,655	$7,321
Sales New Product 1 @ 15% growth	$0	$1,000	$2,300	$2,645	$3,042
Sales New Product 2 @ 10% growth	$0	$0	$750	$1,100	$1,210
Sales New Product 3 @ 10% growth	$0	$0	$0	$4,000	$4,400
Gross Revenue	**$5,000**	**$6,500**	**$9,100**	**$14,400**	**$15,972**
COGs @ 35% of sales	$1,750	$2,275	$3,185	$5,040	$5,590
Gross Profit	**$3,250**	**$4,225**	**$5,915**	**$9,360**	**$10,382**
R&D Expense @ 15% of sales	$750	$975	$1,365	$2,160	$2,396
Non-Recurring R&D Expense	$0	$0	$0	$0	$0
SG&A @ 12% of sales	$600	$780	$1,092	$1,728	$1,917
EBITDA	**$1,900**	**$2,470**	**$3,458**	**$5,472**	**$6,069**

EBITDA is expected to increase from almost $2M in year 1 to $6M in year 5; $19.4M EBITDA cumulatively over the five years. EBITDA as a percent of gross revenue is maintained at 38%. You set the new targets and roll out the plan.

In early February the CTO unexpectedly submits his letter of resignation effective March in year 1. This is not good news. The CTO is a key member of the executive team and is very well respected by employees and throughout the industry. He knows his stuff and there is no one in the organization prepared to step into the role. You have no choice but to hire his replacement from the outside.

The CTO's departure creates havoc with business performance including new product launch delays of six months, forfeiture of 5% annual sales growth across all new products due to unfavorable time to market, the addition of non-recurring R&D expense (such as: time of internal personnel spent on recruiting, search fee, sign on bonus, new hire acclimation and administrative costs, temporary help costs and productivity losses due to the CTO job vacancy, etc.), increases in R&D expense due to loss of departing CTO's expertise, and a 15% increase in base salary needed to close deal with the CTO's replacement. At least there were no costs encountered for the relocation of the new hire or a severance package in the case of involuntary termination of departing CTO.

Lackluster business performance ensues as depicted in Table 1-2.

Table 1-2: Business Performance with CTO Departure

(in thousands)

	Year 1	Year 2	Year 3	Year 4	Year 5
Sales Current Products @ 10% growth	$5,000	$5,500	$6,050	$6,655	$7,321
Sales New Product 1 @ 10% growth	$0	$0	$2,000	$2,200	$2,420
Sales New Product 2 @ 5% growth	$0	$0	$250	$1,050	$1,103
Sales New Product 3 @ 5% growth	$0	$0	$0	$2,000	$4,200
Gross Revenue	**$5,000**	**$5,500**	**$8,300**	**$11,905**	**$15,043**
COGs @ 35% of sales	$1,750	$1,925	$2,905	$4,167	$5,265
Gross Profit	**$3,250**	**$3,575**	**$5,395**	**$7,738**	**$9,778**
R&D Expense @ 15% of sales	$811	$1,038	$1,473	$2,030	$2,519
Non-Recurring R&D Expense	$445	$0	$0	$0	$0
SG&A @ 12% of sales	$600	$660	$996	$1,429	$1,805
EBITDA	**$1,394**	**$1,877**	**$2,926**	**$4,280**	**$5,453**

Compared with the initial business model, the five-year cumulative economic impact is $5M less in revenue and nearly $3.5M less in EBITDA. EBITDA as a percent of gross revenue drops and fluctuates from 27% in year 1 to 36% in year 5.

Now imagine that Murphy's Law takes center stage. The CTO departure snowballs into a host of ailments. The new CTO polarizes the technology team resulting in vast amounts of rework and product launch delays of 18 months, forfeiture of 7% annual sales growth across all new products due to unfavorable time to market, and the escalation of cost of goods sold now equals 40% of sales. The sales team is alienated given several false starts on product launches. A brain drain has begun among the engineers. Where are they flocking to? You guessed it: they have joined the organization that employs your former CTO. Table 1-3 depicts the economic impact.

When comparing this worst case scenario with the initial business model it is clear that business performance has taken a hit, which started with the loss of your former CTO. The original plan called for growing gross revenue from $5M in year 1 to nearly $16M in year 5. Instead revenue grows from $5M in year 1 to $12.5M in year 5. EBITDA was supposed to increase from $1.9M in year 1 to $6M in year 5 but it actually moves from $1.1M in year 1 to $3.8M in year 5; fluctuating between 23% and 31% as a percent of gross revenue. The cumulative losses over the five-year period are staggering. This worst case scenario generates $13M less in revenue and $8.3M less in EBITDA.

Imagine having to deliver that news to your board of directors, shareholders, employees, suppliers, and customers. Publicly traded? Your stock price is on a downward spiral. Need financing for new product development? Think again. Planning to sell the business? There is no way to predict how the disappointing business performance will impact the company valuation. Would not want to be in your shoes.

**Table 1-3: Business Performance with CTO Departure –
Worst Case** (in thousands)

	Year 1	Year 2	Year 3	Year 4	Year 5
Sales Current Products @ 10% annual growth	$5,000	$5,500	$6,050	$6,655	$7,321
Sales New Product 1 @ 8% growth	$0	$0	$0	$2,000	$2,160
Sales New Product 2 @ 3% growth	$0	$0	$0	$250	$1,030
Sales New Product 3 @ 3% growth	$0	$0	$0	$0	$2,000
Gross Revenue	**$5,000**	**$5,500**	**$6,050**	**$8,905**	**$12,511**
COGs @ 40% of sales	$2,000	$2,200	$2,420	$3,562	$5,004
Gross Profit	**$3,000**	**$3,300**	**$3,630**	**$5,343**	**$7,506**
R&D Expense @ 15% of sales	$811	$1,038	$1,136	$1,580	$2,140
Non-Recurring R&D Expense	$445	$0	$0	$0	$0
SG&A @ 12% of sales	$600	$660	$726	$1,069	$1,501
EBITDA	**$1,144**	**$1,602**	**$1,769**	**$2,695**	**$3,865**

The three business models above show how devastating the loss of a key employee can be to an organization that largely grows organically. And any of the three scenarios could occur at your organization too.

SPM – A Tool for M&A

What about company growth through mergers and acquisitions? SPM can be of tremendous value to executives buying and selling businesses. Executives chartered with selling a business can use succession plans as a concrete indicator of business sustainability to prospective buyers. Prospective buyers' interest may peak as they grow more confident in the capabilities and sustainability of the workforce at the target company. And once the deal is done, SPM is a dynamite tool for accelerating how quickly new leaders entering the organization get acquainted with the existing workforce. This would be true regardless of funding or legal structure be it family-owned, venture or private equity backed, public or private.

Never before has there been a more opportune time to beef up talent management practices. SPM is a powerful tool for improving business performance, providing a higher quality employment experience, and proactively addressing projected skills and talent shortages.

Let's add it up. We know:

- The demand for skills and top talent will rise while the supply of top talent will decline.

- Top performing companies choose to proactively address factors over which they have little to no control.

- Many companies sabotage their own growth through the absence of or inadequate talent management practices.

- Knowledge workers expect a high quality employment experience that includes career growth opportunities.

- The loss of key employees can have devastating economic impact on long-term business performance.

- SPM is a confidence builder in companies that grow organically as well as those that grow by merger and acquisition.

Drivers of SPM Among Executives Interviewed

The growing pains experienced by a small to mid-sized company have many upsides and downsides. Filling new positions through internal promotions can become a double-edged sword. On one hand, it's wonderful to provide career growth opportunities to the very folks who contributed to organizational success. On the other hand, the promotional staffing decisions made or approved by executives, who are no longer involved in all external hiring decisions thus less familiar with the talents of newer employees, can be viewed as heavily biased toward the long-service employees with whom they have personal relationships. Conversely, newer employees may be favored because they enter the company with a fresh set of eyes, different experiences and novel approaches.

A number of executives interviewed confided that these "unintentional biases" make their jobs unnecessarily more difficult. A robust, repeatable and objective process allows executives to make or approve key staffing decisions in a way that takes bias out of the equation. Thus they support a more formal SPM process.

During the interviews executives were asked "What triggered SPM in their organizations?" The responses below, while a subset of executives interviewed, are representative of many responses.

The Museum of Science (MOS) in Boston, MA is an example where seven of ten people on the executive team plan to retire over the next five to ten years. The newest member of the team joined over five years ago. Others have 15-plus years tenure. This highly prestigious institution founded in 1830 has some pretty big shoes to fill and has begun the journey of ensuring the torch gets passed to the next generation without a glitch according to its executives who shared their experiences, including Jonathan Burke, Paul Fontaine, and Britton O'Brien.

Kahn, Litwin & Renza Company (KLR), a $35M accounting firm serving middle-market and privately held companies as well as high net worth individuals, has grown organically as well as through acquisition according to Larry Kahn, one of the firm's founders. Now the company prepares to pass the baton to the next generation. This has resulted in a flurry of activity including but not limited to SPM, the founding of its Emerging Leaders Academy as well as thoughtful and deliberate working of its shareholder agreements that govern the terms of retiring partners.

Ipswitch is the maker of software for businesses to manage networks, securely transfer files, and communicate via e-mail. The technologist who wrote the original code and subsequently licensed it to Ipswitch died unexpectedly. While this gentleman was never an Ipswitch employee, his death caused its Chief Executive Officer Roger Greene to pause and contemplate – what is the organization doing to prepare for unexpected disruptions in leadership?

An organization that designs, manufactures and sells medical devices which has grown organically and through acquisition is not new to SPM. One February morning in the earlier part of the 2000 decade, its president had to step down due to a sudden, serious medical condition. When tragedy struck, the remaining executives were prepared to step up thus allowing the board to put the company on the market for sale as planned. The company was successfully sold early the following year. This firm grew from a small standalone company generating under $5M in revenue in the mid 1990s to a division within a global firm with revenue well over $100M in 2012. The current president, promoted from his former position of chief financial officer, met with me in his office to share his experiences.

Paul Kirwin, President and CEO, along with the Chairman of the Board, drive SPM at Northcott Hospitality. Paul had the opportunity to implement SPM and realize its many benefits with his former employer. Needless to say, he made it a top priority after joining Northcott.

A private equity owned $75M manufacturer of custom wire and cable, cable assemblies and coil cords with roughly 400 employees had never done any form of SPM. A SPM playbook, as Frank the new

President put it, would have been tremendously helpful in shortening the amount of time to identify and remedy talent gaps to support company growth goals.

According to past President Greg Baletsa, three business problems demanded Azonix to implement SPM. First was Azonix's high demand for some very specific engineering skills. In fact, the marketplace supply was so limited that search firms wouldn't accept recruiting engagements for these jobs. Second, while positions in lean functions (like finance and human resources) were occupied by seasoned folks, none were ready to take on executive leadership roles. Third, Azonix was established as a standalone entity rather than a division within the Crane Company. While this arrangement afforded Azonix autonomy, it also detracted from Azonix's ability to draw employees from other Crane companies.

Just coming out of the 2008-2009 recession, executives of a 50-year-old company with significant market presence in life sciences and industrials determined through risk planning that talent management was the number one risk to realizing its future growth goals. That prompted the CEO to proceed with succession planning for the top ten executive positions. Six months later the CEO announced his plans for retirement. A new CEO was brought in who also concluded the lean bench strength could impede company growth. So, the new CEO cascaded succession planning further down into the organization and hired a talent management expert to implement its first SPM process.

The personal experience that created the greatest need for SPM over the course of Ken Margossian's career, thus far, was when he was with a large utility company that experienced enormous change and turmoil. Over lunch Ken told me about the New England utility industry and how it was "on fire," in terms of the number of acquisitions made in the 1990s. The consolidation of 22 companies into 7 companies, numerous reorganizations and down-sizings topped off with a successful hostile takeover resulted in cutting $100M in cost in the first two years of the consolidation and reducing headcount from 15,000 employees in 2001 down to 8,000 in 2009. Collectively, these changes rendered the previous succession plans of the 22 companies to no value. Business strategies changed, organization design changed, and jobs changed, as did the capabilities needed to move the organization forward. The only course of action was to create new succession plans for the new combined organization.

In the following pages of this book, these middle-market executives and others whom I will introduce have shared many of their lessons learned as it relates to people succession.

Footnotes

1. Bergeron Associates™ and Insight Management Group, *Enterprise Performance Management Study - Executive Summary*, 2006.

2. AICPA & CIMA, CGMA Report: *Talent Pipeline Draining Growth - Connecting human capital to the growth agenda*, September 2012.

3. Boston Consulting Group, *People Management Translated into Superior Economic Performance*, August 2012.

4. Blessing White, *Employee Engagement Report 2011 - Beyond the numbers: a practical approach for individuals, managers, and executives*, 2011.

5. Right Management Inc., *Employee Engagement - Maximizing Organizational Performance*, 2009.

HIGHLIGHTS

- The demand for skills and top talent will rise while the supply of top talent will decline.

- Top performing companies choose to proactively address factors over which they have little to no control.

- Many companies sabotage their own growth through the absence of or inadequate talent management practices.

- Knowledge workers expect a high quality employment experience that includes career growth opportunities.

- The loss of key employees can have devastating economic impact on long-term business performance.

- SPM is a confidence builder in companies that grow organically as well as those that grow by merger and acquisition.

- SPM is no longer reserved for large companies; middle-market companies can do a credible job too if they so choose.

- Middle-market companies initiate SPM for reasons such as:
  o Expected talent loss due to reasons such as retirement
  o Unexpected talent loss due to termination, disablement or death
  o The desire to build leadership and mission critical capability bench strength to achieve growth goals
  o The need to develop an internal talent pool given difficulties recruiting from the external talent pool
  o Expansion of specific expertise needed to support growth such as mergers & acquisitions and business unit management expertise

Chapter 2
People Succession Defined

Some of the executive experiences shared in this book occurred in middle-market companies that had a formal succession planning & management (SPM) process. Other experiences occurred in firms that had no formal SPM in place. Yet the goals, convictions, challenges and actions from both groups demonstrate a practical application of SPM yielding career growth and advancement of people ready to take on new roles. This chapter provides an overview of the phases in a formal SPM process so that readers connect insights reported by the executives interviewed, and understand the interdependencies between the individual and collective importance of the phases.

Succession Planning & Management Defined

Succession planning (SP) is a process used to identify high performing internal candidates who have the potential to fill talent needs required to ensure long-term organizational success. SP includes defining talent needs in a useful way, objectively assessing people against those needs and identifying people who have potential to meet the needs.

For example, workforce analysis may reveal that nearly every member of your executive team is planning to retire within a five-year window. Thus, your SPM objective is to proactively prepare people to step into the executive roles. You focus initially on assessing director level management. Situational analysis and talent assessment reveals that director level employees are not as strategy-focused as an executive job would demand. That prompts the question, "Why?" Turns out middle-management and supervisory layoffs left the directors with little time to do anything other than manage at the operational and tactical levels. The question then becomes "Which directors are capable of becoming far more strategic-minded?" Won't know until you try. Your SP initially consists of giving all directors an initial assignment of delegating work. This frees up their time for new projects intended to stretch and develop their strategic thinking capabilities.

Succession planning alone is insufficient. It must be augmented with succession management (SM), which is simply the day-to-day effort involved in preparing people for different responsibilities. Succession management encompasses building the capabilities and confidence needed from people now and in the future.

Back to the example, preparing people for executive positions may include a mix of experiential work assignments that mimic responsibilities in the targeted executive positions, debriefs, coaching, mentoring, and training on strategic thinking approaches followed by a job change such as function head, business unit manager or country manager expatriate assignment.

Combined, SPM is a hugely powerful talent solution for positioning the organization for future success. First, it solves the problem of supplying the organization with much of its needed talent. And given the predicted domestic and global talent shortages that is significant. Second, it reduces the risk of business disruptions and organizational underperformance due to job vacancies or key positions occupied by people who are not fully prepared.

SPM is not reserved for the executive suite anymore. It includes jobs at any level in the organization that require specific knowledge and expertise critical to the organization's success (i.e. mission critical skills and capabilities). When SPM is first implemented, organizations tend to focus on leadership positions. That's a fine start, but organizations must dive deeper and cover all mission critical roles. The broader application of SPM strengthens the overall workforce. Omitting other mission critical capabilities regardless of the level of the organization in which they reside, could cripple a company. Answering several questions can help avoid this grave error of omission. Consider:

- What absence of capabilities would make it difficult to achieve organizational growth goals? Realize vision? Deliver on the customer value proposition? Leave room for capabilities such as: leadership, expertise – technical or otherwise - and externally focused relationship capabilities.

For each capability:

- How critical is the capability to executing the business strategy?

- How difficult is it to recruit external candidates with the capability?

- How difficult is it to develop internal candidates with the capability?

The SPM Process

SPM (Figure 2-1), designed as a robust, repeatable process, includes: setting goals and scope to support the execution of the business strategy; defining talent needs and mission critical capabilities; inventorying existing talent capabilities; making informed workforce investment decisions; proactively preparing people for future responsibilities; making informed deployment decisions; and measuring progress.

Educating the people managers expected to execute the SPM process is critical to success for a host of reasons. First, employment decisions made within the context of SPM are subject to employment regulations just as are other employment decisions. Decisions must be objective, fair, valid and legally defensible and analogous to the approaches used for hiring external candidates. When in doubt, consult an employment attorney.

A second reason for educating people managers is to convey practical approaches for implementation within the context of your organization, its business objectives, mission critical capabilities, core values and culture. Frankly, most managers understand the concepts associated with "getting people ready" for career advancement. Some lack proficiency applying them on a day-to-day basis. And the nuances in how your organization applies the concepts may differ from those of past employers of your people managers. For organizations implementing SPM for the first time, integrate SPM training into the change management approach used to implement SPM uniformly across the organization.

A third reason to educate people managers on SPM is to communicate performance expectations of both the SPM program itself and the people managers responsible for implementation. It is not at all uncommon to make SPM objectives part of each manager's performance plan or bonus earning criteria as a concrete way to reinforce, reward or penalize SPM results generated by the manager. Remember, SPM is a risk management tool for economic sustainability of the organization. It makes sense to grab the people managers' attention through risk/reward approaches. Plus with compensation at stake, it solidifies SPM as a legitimate business imperative.

Figure 2-1: Succession Planning & Management Process

When embarking on the SPM process be sure to distinguish between current and future talent needs of the organization. The focus on current needs positions you to address short-term challenges while the focus on future needs positions you to address long-term challenges. You need to plan for both.

1. Set Goals and Scope

As with any new initiative, establishing the goals and scope of SPM are best established up-front so as to avoid boiling the ocean or costly errors of omission. Goals and scope may be expressed in terms of the mission critical skills needed, the quantity required over a finite period of time, the organizational level in which they are to reside and how they link to the achievement of business objectives.

Undoubtedly the analyses and conversations that lead to setting goals and scope will depend on whether your SPM is designed to orchestrate replacement succession or build a talent pipeline. The former involves preparing a successor for an existing role which may satisfy a short-term talent need such as retirement of an existing incumbent. It may not, however, take into account changes in talent needs due to a host of external and internal factors. The latter approach, building a talent pipeline or bench strength, is a solution that adapts to dynamic factors. Most organizations will elect a dual approach so that both short and long-term talent needs are proactively addressed.

 Example: A 50-year-old company in life sciences and industrials, found an executive thinking exercise, or scenario planning, to be of great value. The exercise asks executives to imagine that the business has been decimated. Then executives are asked to identify what killed it? What could have been done to prevent it? What kind of capabilities would be required of the workforce to prevent it? Working through the scenario helped the company to set SPM goals and scope of positions covered.

In pushing strategic thinking further, you might compare and contrast two scenarios. For example, in Scenario 1, the business was decimated by the competition, an external factor. In Scenario 2, business failure resulted from the organization's inability to promptly execute on its strategy due to internal factors. Ask executives to answer similar drill down questions for both scenarios. Then look for commonality. Also, think through the probability of either scenario playing out. Start creating your SP from there.

2. Define Talent Needs

The fundamental principle in this step is to define your talent needs up-front and then write them down in suffiicient detail so that people managers and employees understand the capabilities to be developed. Plus it provides a basis from which to align all the remaining steps in the SPM process.

Defining talent expectations is a prerequisite for assembling the right mix of people to achieve business objectives. The definitions must be specific enough so that employees and their managers can easily gauge strengths and areas of development, a must have when embarking on SPM, and the basis from which Step 3 is performed.

🕐 **Time Saver:** Prepared well, the talent definitions are integrated into other talent strategy components and may be repurposed for: setting performance expectations, recruiting external candidates, establishing learning objectives in workshops and the like.

The written definitions may take a variety of forms including – my favorite – the leadership profile. Sometimes called a competency model, the leadership profile conveys the attributes, behaviors, skills and knowledge expected and needed of people aspiring to leadership positions. Reflecting on what your star performers do differently than others in similar roles is a good place to start when creating a leadership profile. For best results, align definitions with company goals, values, and design, and customize for level within the organization. The same principles apply when creating competency profiles for mission critical jobs that are not leadership specific.

3. Inventory Existing Talent Capabilities

Objectively assess employees against the defined talent needs. Areas of strength, improvement, and development opportunities can be determined for each individual as well as collectively across the organization.

This step includes the culmination of other employee-specific inputs commonly gleaned from: resumes for an overview of past experiences and achievements, performance records and career conversations between managers and their employees to ascertain employee passions, desire for development, career growth aspirations, and interest in mobility.

Executives begin putting the pieces of the puzzle together by taking into account defined talent needs and the results of the employee inventory.

Time Saver: Get people managers to partner with Human Resources so that they work together one-on-one on both inventorying employee capabilities (Step 3 in SPM) and creating actionable development plans (Step 5 in SPM). Continuity across the organization is greater. Momentum is sustained. People managers' time is conserved.

4. Make Investment Decisions

The next step is for company executives to gather in a forum often called a "talent review." The talent review allows executives to get better acquainted with the collective talent pool, calibrate similar performance and potential assessments across the organization, and decide on development priorities and investments to be made.

Below are several guidelines for executives looking to get the most from their talent reviews:

- Educate executives on the talent review agenda, their roles and responsibilities before, during and after the talent reviews, and expected outcomes.

- Start the session by reviewing business direction, resulting talent needs and status of supply versus demand of those talent needs.

- Establish a common definition of potential used by all managers for calibrating employees across the organization; sooner rather than later makes for a more efficient SPM process.

- Executives share highlights of each employee including information gathered through Step 3. Potential future assignments are discussed and may include: promotions (vertical), transfers (horizontal), job rotations, special assignments (such as an expatriate assignment), expansion of responsibilities in current role, and special projects intended to broaden experience, and exposure to people and functions that solve real business problems.

- Once calibration of potential and performance is done, then executives set development priorities and make investment decisions. Get specific on the forms of development to be used and respective timeframes.

- Remind executives that performance and potential ratings of individual employees change over time.

The session fosters conversation on desirable on-the-job development assignments regardless of where in the organization the employees and the assignments reside. As employees complete experiential work assignments and more talent reviews occur, familiarity with the strengths, performance and promise of any one employee will grow exponentially among the executives. And that is indispensible for making informed talent deployment decisions (Step 7).

It is worth pointing out that talent review sessions create focus on SPM and produce tangible development plans. But don't hesitate to integrate "talent" agenda items into other management meetings. This practice reinforces the importance of proactively managing talent risks, alongside other business risks, and helps build momentum on implementing action items. The output of this phase is the succession plan.

Time Saver: Host daylong talent reviews rather than a series of shorter reviews to maintain momentum. Host quarterly talent review updates to verify progress on employee development, dole out more experiential work assignments, and monitor SPM results.

5. Prepare People

Solidify individual development plans during this step. Development plans include: development goals; resources and initiatives required in preparing the employee for achieving each goal; and experiential work assignments for learning, improving, and eventually mastering capabilities needed by the organization.

Additional assessments may be used as part of setting development goals in this step or an earlier one. They range from the assessment of thinking styles, emotional intelligence or personality to 360° feedback based on input from the employee's manager, direct reports and peers. Assessments are a wonderful way for establishing employee awareness on areas of strength and improvement and prelude to development activities. However simple or sophisticated organizations get on their use of assessments, choose them thoughtfully, verify their suitability for SPM, and use them consistently for best results.

Chapter 8, Talent Magnet Tool Kit, offers a wide range of talent preparation venues. Mix and match the most effective approaches in a way that fits your organization's wallet. Within the context of SPM, the venues chosen for any one individual are chosen on the basis of individual development goals. The most critical component to any employee's development plan is some form of experiential work assignment or on-the-job training.

 Example: A $650M digital audio and video solutions company expects its people managers to meet with direct reports at least once every two weeks to discuss project status and progress made toward career growth and development goals. To create accountability an annual employee survey asks employees "Have you had meetings with your manager every two weeks?" The manager receives summarized feedback for his/her area of responsibility as well as in comparison to other managers.

Time Saver: If career coaching sessions once every two weeks is unreasonable, then adapt and make it once a month. People managers will figure out the frequency and rhythm of sessions required to generate expected results.

6. Make Talent Deployment Decisions

When key roles need to be filled, whether due to planned or unplanned job vacancies, restructuring, or planned growth, executives now have a powerful tool to help identify who among existing employees are the most qualified and promising candidates. Hiring an external replacement is no longer the only option!

Because the executive has greater familiarity with a wider range of employees, the list of internal candidates spans well beyond employees in his/her direct area of responsibility.

Calling a special talent review session with the executives who crafted the original succession plan provides a confidential forum for thinking through the options. No doubt situational factors and the impact to the organization as well as other key stakeholders will be considered prior to making a deployment decision. Once a selection has been made then discussion focuses on how to best prepare and transition the employee into the new role and who will fill his/her job vacancy, if needed. Peer executive input is invaluable. It's important for shared ownership in decisions and their successful implementation.

 Example: The unexpected departure of an Ipswitch division head prompted CEO Roger Greene to fill the position with an external candidate. Unfortunately, that candidate did not work out. Roger's next deployment decision involved asking the next most senior person to lead the division on an interim basis while simultaneously starting a search for a new external candidate. The employee accepted knowing full well that a search was initiated.

Long story short, the interim manager did a wonderful job, which showed up in the business results generated by his team. The interim manager's passion for the work and ability to create a great working environment inspired the team, thereby furthering their success and acceptance of him as their leader. Roger's next deployment decision was to formalize the full-time promotion of the leader. Roger also committed to developing internal candidates so that the diamonds in the rough won't be overlooked when making future deployment decisions.

7. Measure Progress

As with any program worth doing, monitoring and measuring quantitative and qualitative results is important so that:

- Momentum continues to build through early demonstration of small and consecutive wins.

- A healthy return on investment fuels the continuance of SPM.

- People take ownership for their responsibilities in SPM.

- There is early identification of what works and what doesn't.

- Rapid adjustments are made to create greater value through SPM.

Example: The $650M digital audio and video solutions company – At the six month mark after a new successor takes the helm, the executive checks-in with both the successor and his/her direct reports. With the successor, changes to his/her on-boarding plan are discussed to recognize that six months into the new assignment may have prompted additional insights. Feedback is solicited via a 360° feedback assessment from the successor's new direct reports. Monitoring like this helps get things back of track if need be.

HIGHLIGHTS

- Succession planning must be augmented with succession management to effectively build the capabilities and confidence needed from employees now and in the future.

- SPM is no longer reserved for executive leadership roles. Identify all mission critical capabilities or roles which may include leadership, expertise – technical or otherwise – and externally focused relationship capabilities.

- Be sure to distinguish current from future mission critical capabilities.

- Educating people managers expected to execute the SPM process is a critical success factor.

- Build a SPM process that is simple, robust, and repeatable because SPM is a process and not an event.

- SPM includes: setting goals and scope to support the execution of the business strategy; defining talent needs and mission critical capabilities; inventorying existing talent capabilities; making informed workforce investment decisions; proactively preparing people for future responsibilities; making informed deployment decisions; and measuring progress.

Chapter 3

The School of Hard Knocks

Now that we've walked through a formal SPM process, the question moves from "How do you go about doing SPM?" to "Will you choose to do SPM in your middle-market company, and if so, why?"

Sometimes, executives learn the value of SPM the hard way. This chapter consists of a few unforgettable hard knock stories that motivated the executives to make SPM a priority throughout their careers. Their early career experiences illuminate why they value SPM and use SPM to shape how they go about preparing employees for new roles and responsibilities.

The Near Death Experience

Imagine you are the chief information officer (CIO) for a $1.2B injection molding and contract manufacturing firm with 66 locations across 18 countries. This is a pretty big job; however, as CIO you aspire to become a member of the small cadre of executives who make strategic decisions for the company. Conversations about your ultimate career aspiration have been limited to your immediate boss. The discussions identified some development areas, but the feedback was too general for purposes of preparing for a membership role on the executive leadership team. A concrete discussion on the gaps between your current and desired responsibilities and skill would have brought much more clarity to development planning.

Now imagine that you, the CIO, along with one hundred of the company's senior leaders, file into a large conference room for the president's executive update. Many executives have traveled from afar to attend this quarterly session at headquarters. Therefore, the coffee station adjacent to the conference room serves an important function – to encourage you and peers to reconnect and strengthen relationships. After some networking, everyone is directed to take their seats and the session begins.

This forum is unique because it's the first hosted by the company's new president. The new president sets the tone with comments like "We are here to confront the brutal truths about what is wrong with the company." And despite his invitation to speak openly and without repercussion, as the session progresses your feelings of frustration grow. You cannot shake the nagging feeling that speaking candidly is nothing more than a naïve notion.

The next thing you know you stand up and verbally assault the new president. Your loud booming voice and flailing arms could not be mistaken for playing the role of devil's advocate, expressing a difference of opinion, or engaging in debate. No, you pulled out all the stops and really sailed into the president in front of one hundred of your colleagues. You crossed the line. The president allowed you to finish your rant, then took back control of the meeting and pressed on. When the session broke for coffee, none of your colleagues would look you in the eye let alone speak with you, even those whom you considered to be friends. They avoided you like the plague.

The internal dialogue in your head got stuck on replay: "you are toast, you are going to be fired, your career is dead and you will never ever get hired again!"

This is the true story of Jay Leader during his time at Nypro Inc. This "near death experience" changed his life. So, what did he do? Later that same day Jay sought out the new president and apologized. Further, he took full responsibility for his action and said he was prepared to accept the consequences. After all, Jay acknowledged, "the president was well within his right to fire me." But he didn't. Instead, Jay was offered executive coaching where emotional intelligence was a focus. He willingly accepted. The forum incident, the olive branch extended by the president, and the coaching changed his life.

With a lot of reflection and hard work, Jay eventually achieved his career aspiration as a member of the executive team responsible for making strategic decisions for the company first in the role of CIO with iRobot then again with Rapid7. The near death experience influenced how he goes about developing his people. Emotional and social intelligence and influence are at the top of the development list for those preparing for executive roles. You will learn more about Jay's approach to debriefing his folks before and after important interactions with stakeholders in Chapter 5. The 1 - 2 - 3 Debrief is one of the most valuable learning venues that Jay consistently uses.

Bootstrapping within a Corporate Setting

Iron Mountain's second largest vertical business, Healthcare, which generates in excess of $350M in revenue within the $3B global services company, started like most other businesses do – as a business line. Running the profit and loss center of the business line, when it consisted of about 13% of company revenue, was one of the most challenging assignments General Manager Ken Rubin ever had. The mix of fully dedicated resources and those shared with others in the company made the job especially challenging. Influencing, cajoling and negotiating resources internally consumed much of his time. Ken's efforts paid off as the business line moved from worst to first place, graduated to business unit stature and earned him the General Manager/Senior Vice President role.

Ken's 20/20 hindsight of bootstrapping resources throughout the matrixed organization continues to serve him well when preparing future business line managers within his organization. You see, today the Healthcare business unit is comprised of just over 100 fully dedicated customer facing, product management, operational and marketing professionals. Like other businesses at Iron Mountain, Healthcare relies on the central operations organization for many services. For Healthcare the number of partially dedicated employees in core operations is in the hundreds. Ken's goal is to make the transition from business line manager to General Manager in a heavily matrixed organization easier on future employees. Chapter 5 elaborates on how Ken prepares employees for the new roles.

HIGHLIGHTS

- Reflect on what you learned from the most challenging professional situations and blunders faced over your career.

- Share your experiences and the resulting insights with others.

- Select development venues that position you to debrief, coach, and mentor employees so they are better prepared when traveling similar career paths.

People Succession

Chapter 4

Career Champions

In this chapter, several executives look back on their own career advancement, how those experiences underscore their commitment to SPM and the importance of talent management practices used today in their own SPM efforts.

Peer Mentoring

The story of Judy Nitsch and Lisa Brothers started over twenty-five years ago when they worked together at the same civil engineering services company. Judy was a director with civil engineering, marketing, business development, and client relations responsibilities and expertise. She is naturally energized by networking and relationship building. Meanwhile, Lisa developed considerable skills in construction and operations.

When Judy announced her plans to leave and form her own company in 1989, Lisa immediately sought Judy out to pursue a career opportunity. Lisa knew Judy would succeed and that Judy's collaborative style clicked better than that of her then current employer. Given the limitations imposed by a non-solicitation agreement, Judy's hands had been tied; but because Lisa had approached her, Lisa could join Judy's new firm without penalty. Six months after Judy's departure, Lisa joined Nitsch Engineering – a firm that specializes in civil engineering, land surveying, transportation engineering, sustainable site consulting, planning, and geographic information systems.

Their complimentary skills, firm belief in people as a source of competitive advantage and ability to execute, poised Nitsch Engineering for its robust growth. Lisa earned an MBA and was engaged and mentored by Judy with their long-term plan being Lisa's eventual promotion to chief operating officer, then to president and chief executive officer. As their learning, trust and experience grew, the two women engaged regularly in peer coaching. Today, Judy's title is Founding Principal and she concentrates on business development and client relations; she continues to be the Chairman of the Board.

Ambition and the desire to learn are prerequisites to investing in one's personal development. Peer coaching and mentoring are development venues among others that Lisa employs daily as a way to prepare employees for future responsibilities given their informal SPM. It worked for her; and employees, regardless of generation, really take to it. Judy says she has learned much from Lisa over the years as well.

Ambition is a Good Thing

The president of ABC Company, let's call her Cindy, has been responsible for the one billion dollar joint venture owned by two Fortune 100 companies since 2009. The organization was formed in the mid-1990s and designs, manufactures, and services high technology capital equipment serving commercial markets. When I stopped by to interview Cindy, she had just wrapped up a quarterly session with one of the 15 employees whom she mentors at her firm.

Cindy has an amazing track record of career advancement. She was hired 29 years ago by one of ABC Company's parent companies as an executive assistant working in government relations. Her recall of pivotal career conversations with her boss and his boss was impressive – as though it happened just yesterday. The conversations contributed to owning the responsibility for her own career management, the importance of recognizing her strengths, and working with trusted, savvy mentors. Rather than be swayed to join another company in a similar job as her next career move, her boss encouraged her to apply for a job where she would write speeches for the company president. Admittedly, this career move was not on her radar screen; however, the move provided a network building opportunity among executives.

Environment, Health and Safety, a valued function within the company, was her next stop. Cindy freely admits that, looking back, this was not her best career move. It did not play to her passion, strengths and preference for customer/external versus internally focused responsibilities.

Next, she pursued an externally oriented role in contracts where she worked very closely with the sales team on contract terms and conditions. Her migration to a sales road warrior position, while a natural segue from contracts, required addressing three issues head on. First, she made upper management aware of her interest in the job – the easy part in a company with a formal SPM process. Second, since Cindy is not engineer educated it took some reassurances that she'd move up the technology learning curve quickly. Third, addressing work/life balance concerns (at a time when there was only one other woman on the sales force) took courage and persistence which paid off.

Was there ever a job that got away? Yes! Cindy threw her hat into the ring for a leadership role with an affiliated joint venture company. She didn't land the role. Despite her disappointment, it wasn't long before she was approached for a senior management role in Europe with responsibilities for sales, marketing, customer support, and program management.

After three years Cindy moved back to the states for the top marketing job followed by her current role as president at ABC Company. An interesting nuance to her new responsibilities in operations and program management is getting employees from two fierce competitors and parent companies to work in unity. There is never a dull moment and Cindy loves it that way!

To what does Cindy attribute her success in moving from executive assistant to president of a technology company without the benefit of a technical degree? At the top of the list is open communication with senior management about her career aspirations, not being afraid to dig in and learn and ask questions, selecting roles that play to her strengths, delivering results, networking, and mentoring. Now on the other side of the table, Cindy uses all of these approaches and more when executing on succession plans.

Preventing Poachers

Ken Rubin, General Manager of the Healthcare vertical at Iron Mountain shared the compelling story of a woman – let's call her Sally – who pursued a director job opening that was two levels above her then current job. Given the importance of the role, Ken proactively sourced top applicants and considered a number of solid internal candidates as well as some talented external ones before learning of Sally's interest.

Admittedly Ken's first inclination was to politely dismiss Sally as a candidate for the director role. He'd not taken that kind of risk with anyone to date. Jumping up job levels created risk not just for Sally but for the organization as well. Plus he had a pool of reasonably qualified candidates. Sally persisted and earned an interview. Ken was impressed and more comfortably moved forward with Sally as a candidate. As part of his hiring due diligence, Ken explored Sally's track record at the company discovering that she repeatedly produced impressive results, worked well with and was respected by others, knew her stuff and came across as strong and confident with all who interviewed her. Ken was delighted to offer her the job and Sally accepted enthusiastically.

After eight or nine months of outstanding job performance Sally completed her MBA, where she was being schooled alongside C-level executives of other firms. Ken started to worry that this fast tracker could become a flight risk if wooed away by a peer graduate student so he deliberately assigned her new, exciting and highly visible projects sooner rather than later.

Ken's takeaway is that executives must be receptive to career advancement inquiries made of its brightest employees regardless of what level on the organization chart they fall. Had he not listened and given Sally serious consideration then his divisional performance could have suffered and the company could have lost one of its most valuable future leaders.

HIGHLIGHTS

Strategies for advancing one's career include:

- Produce great results.

- Proactively pursue several career paths – even those that are not an obvious choice.

- Make career choices based on your passion, strengths, and opportunity to work with people from whom you can learn.

- Be professional when dealing with disappointment such as when the ideal job gets away.

- Commit to lifelong learning in its many forms.

- Build a strong network of trusted coaches, mentors, and professionals with "can do" approaches, competence and connections.

Strategies for middle-market executives embarking on SPM:

- Coach employees on the above strategies for furthering their career advancement.

- Keep an open mind when it comes to identifying your organization's future leaders early in their careers.

- Populate your organization at every level with effective coaches and mentors.

Chapter 5

Climate Counts

Have you ever been selected to champion a new methodology, let's say lean principles, and began your journey by attending outside training followed by independent study and research? From there you were expected to carry the torch from vision-setting clear through implementation at your company. That's a pretty daunting task for an individual, especially if your organization does not adapt well to change. Or perhaps you transferred from one division to another within your firm. Even though all the divisions share core values, you learn the hard way that your tried and true approaches do not work in the new division. Those are but a few situations that executives implementing SPM must address and this chapter arms you with a few solutions.

1 – 2 – 3 Debrief

Jay Leader, near death survivor and currently CIO of Rapid7, employs the 1 - 2 - 3 Debrief when preparing future leaders among his most promising performers. Remember, his "ah-ha" moment came at great expense and in front of his peers. He wouldn't wish that near death experience on anyone. Fortunately his boss did not give up on him and that left quite an impression. Today Jay does not give up on good people. Instead he works with those who have enough of the right stuff (including the willingness to learn and apply what they've learned) while working toward a common goal. And while his folks are mostly information technology professionals, much of the wisdom he imparts is focused on how to build relationships, influence stakeholders, anticipate obstacles, and adapt to the political environment.

How does he do it? Step 1 of his 1 – 2 – 3 Debrief is rehearsing a meeting before it happens. This is especially true for those meetings with executive visibility, where the stakes are high or there is already much controversy. It includes (a) articulating desired outcomes, (b) creating an approach for achieving those outcomes that takes into account executive mindset, competing priorities, and anticipated resistance, and (c) some role playing. Step 2 is the meeting itself. And in Step 3 he and his staff debrief on the meeting, identifying the executives' thinking processes and concerns, meeting navigation tactics, questioning techniques, and other behaviors. The combination of these steps gets his folks thinking in terms of the context in which they operate. Their broadened thinking patterns become blatantly apparent in future sessions when employees compare and contrast new situations to past ones then adapt their approaches. It takes time to get people to objectively observe the meetings they attend, but it works and is well worth the investment.

General Management Preparation

Ken Rubin, General Manager of the Healthcare vertical at Iron Mountain, applied what he learned when having to muster up partially dedicated resources across the company to fuel his organization's growth. His hard knocks story left a substantial impression. His overarching goal is to provide his promising performers the knowledge, tools, support, and environment so they can navigate and recruit resources across the company. After all, achieving company goals, business unit goals, and individual advancement goals depend upon it.

Ken uses a series of learning forums when preparing future General Managers. Among his learners are people who are technically competent in their respective fields but still have much to study when it comes to leading people in a matrixed organization. The role Ken plays in the forums is that of mentor, coach, facilitator, and supporter. Here is his roughed out game plan:

- Early on Ken works with each potential general manager on setting a clear vision, direction and high level strategy for the assigned business area.

- In tandem, Ken hosts a series of routine one-on-one check-ins with all the GM wannabees that go well beyond discussing milestones in the business strategy. They often revolve around navigating and influencing people in and around the organization.

- He supports the employee's efforts in securing a strong business team comprised of fully and partially dedicated members.

- He supports the creation of monthly business review sessions attended by all business team members, fully and partially dedicated, to keep all the heads in the game. The sessions operate as a pulpit from which the new leader influences strategy and its execution, builds strong mutually rewarding relationships and celebrates successes both large and small.

- In addition, Ken encourages the new leader to create her own stakeholder management plan requiring monthly one-on-one check-ins with each business team member as well as stakeholders not on the team. This step is designed to strengthen relationships and influence when needed.

- Ken, with each new leader, conducts occasional business team debrief sessions to close out events, recognize milestone achievement and/or devise mid-course corrections as needed. These sessions generate much learning not just by the new leader but by all business team members too.

When preparing future leaders of the organization executives must be well intentioned, genuine, open, consistent, and helpful in all situations before, during and after pivotal learning experiences. This way, no matter how things play out for better or for worse (be it advancement, temporary setback, or even termination) the employee knows and trusts the executive.

Set the Stage

Dave Mallen, Partner of The Wilder Companies, a retail real estate development, management and leasing second generation family owned firm, recalls a time when there was an imbalance of perceived value of the finance and accounting function. And given the thrust of the company's business deals that imbalance created unnecessary self-inflicted problems and operational inefficiencies. Correcting the imbalance first required executive commitment in terms of both consistent communications and action. For instance, it was up to executives to set the expectation that finance would participate in pivotal meetings to get deals done. The meetings became learning forums for the business as well as the finance leaders. They served as opportunities to understand each other's thought processes and get creative by mixing and matching ideas that best served customers. Eventually the "partnering" took hold resulting in finance's elevated status demonstrated by their being sought out regularly by their business manager counterparts. Now that the bar has been raised it is up to finance and accounting to maintain their higher status by constantly improving their leadership, relationship, influence, and creative problem solving skills. Executive support comes in many forms regardless of where the employees are along the leadership learning curve.

HIGHLIGHTS

- Select promising performers who are highly motivated. For promising performers generating results, the desire for learning, ambition, and passion for their work is the winning combination.

- Select people managers who possess the promising performer traits and have passion for helping others become successful. Hire people managers who enjoy developing, coaching, and mentoring others. If they haven't yet established a track record for developing people, as is commonly the case among technical talent, but want to learn and understand what they will be held accountable for, then go for it.

- Lead by example.

- Use a range of one-on-one and group forums in which effective, sustainable, and trustful learning approaches occur.

- Teach what not to do as well as what to do.

- Build trust through one-on-one relationships. Folks disregard feedback and decline coaching and mentoring invitations from people whom they do not trust. Focus on creating an environment in which conversations between people managers and employees are frequent, fluid, trust-filled, and focused on shared goals.

- Tolerate mistakes because that is how people learn and often segues into creative and innovative solutions. Define tolerable levels of risk, and encourage learning from the experiences and applying those lessons to future situations.

Chapter 6

Derail the Derailers

An effective people succession plan in a nutshell answers the question: Who will lead your organization in the future? Regardless of the horizon for which you are planning, be it one, three or five plus years out, it is important to understand and mitigate potential derailers. By derailers I mean perceptions or beliefs used for not doing SPM. Without everyone on board, inaction is sure to push SPM off track. Pay special attention to the potential derailers posed by the managers ultimately responsible for preparing your future leaders – the people managers. Resistance or hesitation on their part may be overt and/or covert. Understanding why resistance exists and the forms that it takes is the first step toward overcoming the derailers. The remaining steps may require change management practices that at a minimum will depend on your starting point, established trust levels in the company, culture, and severity of talent gaps.

Derailer 1: SPM Takes Too Much Time

Many of the executives interviewed disclosed that day-to-day operations are nearly all-consuming resulting in insufficient time and resources dedicated to SPM. This was especially true when preparing employees for different responsibilities.

Remember:

- Preparation work and development are at the heart of SPM. And study after study shows that employee development favorably impacts employee engagement and retention levels as well as organizational productivity and profitability. Anything you can do to increase employee development investments relevant to your firm is a win-win.

- SPM is part of risk management and planning. If left unaddressed and something goes wrong, then corrective action will demand exponentially more money from the organization and time from you.

Dealing with this derailer calls for:

Making time by taking something off your plate; so delegate. Delegating is one of the most impactful ways to develop others for future responsibilities and free up your own time!

Derailer 2: SPM is Unimportant

A few executives invited to participate in an interview for this book had comments like "I usually wait until the last minute, then whip something up so that I can check off the box indicating to Human Resources that I completed it. So, I might not be the right executive to interview as I spend very little time on it." Interpretation – SPM is not of value and so I exert the least amount of energy as possible on it.

Other executives interviewed commented on a number of potential derailers expressed by their people managers, such as: "it conflicts with my time and attention needed to work on real business issues," "it's an HR program," "it's a waste of time," "I just hire new people when needed." Or you won't hear a peep from executives and they just delay, delay, delay in completing SPM related requests. If these folks reside in your organization then your company's succession plan may be compromised. Furthermore, employees notice when leadership fails to "walk the talk."

Dealing with this derailer calls for:

- Strong executive leadership that: believes people are a critical source of competitive advantage, walks the talk, provides clarity on SPM expectations of executives and people managers, and ensures short and long-term talent management goals are communicated, measured, and monitored like other important business goals.

- Working with the doubters on their own career advancement so they have a positive first-hand experience.

- Understanding what is driving the defeatist attitude and addressing it. Could previous experiences with SPM be tainting enthusiasm? What about thinking styles – particularly as it relates to short versus long-term perspectives? How about core values and belief systems among the naysayers? Or could complacency be the driver?

- Changing the mindset. Doubting Thomases may be surprised to learn how their counterparts in and outside the company are effectively leveraging SPM as a critical tool in business goal achievement and their own career advancement.

- Building a robust, repeatable and simple SPM program.

- Reinforcing people manager accountability for achievement of SPM goals through a mix of carrot and the stick approaches.

- When recruiting new people managers, hire those who have passion and a track record for developing themselves and others along with other required skills.

These approaches are applicable to a wide range of SPM derailers not just Derailer 2.

Derailer 3: SPM Poses a Threat to Job Security

Another reason why people managers may resist SPM is the threat of their own job security. What if they develop promising performers who ultimately replace them? This fear is very real and cuts to the core of professional survival, which can become magnified in a lousy job market. Ask yourself:

- Did the people manager ever experience job loss or other professional disappointment after developing his/her successor at your firm or a previous one?

- In preparing a past successor did the people manager get freed up to make his/her own advancement opportunity a reality?

- How high is the trust level between you and the people manager?

Act 1: You are hired as a top executive by a $1.5B global company that utilizes matrix management. After a series of discussions throughout the hiring process, you expect that as you move through progressively more responsible positions you will undoubtedly tap into your vast general management, merger and acquisition and leadership experience in transitioning the organization from a decentralized to a centralized structure.

Act 2: Once on board you are asked to review the executive playbook as fully expected. After careful analysis of the business model, strategy, and proposed central structure you craft a series of conclusions and recommendations to position the company for desired future growth. Your most significant conclusion is that the model for centralization is premature. It will work once the organization hits a much higher revenue mark. Under-resourcing the products with greatest potential, per the playbook, will result in stunting organizational growth. Your suggestions are not well received despite repeated attempts to influence on the basis of optimizing organizational growth and performance. The company executes its playbook, and sure enough, the company's growth goals go unachieved.

Act 3: As the only person on the eight person executive team with mergers and acquisitions experience, you are chartered with leading acquisition activity, reviewing 75 target companies resulting in 6 actual acquisitions. Additionally, as a true believer in developing people, you educate your executive counterparts on the legal and financial matters and tools and techniques of due diligence. Acquisition activity was fast and furious for a while but died off in 2008-2009, at which time your role changed to General Manager of a division.

Act 4: In your new role as General Manager, you are assigned responsibility and accountability for running a profitable business in addition to developing the merger and acquisition and business skills of the top two people in the division, neither of whom report to you. Your reward for catapulting the organization onto an accelerated growth track and developing the two leaders was a demotion; you now report to one of the two fellows you educated.

This is but one of several experiences that a seasoned executive, let's call him George, shared with me over lunch at a local library. The moral of this story is to get crystal clear on what roles employees are being groomed for and their development plans. This is true of future leaders as well as the people managers facilitating their development. Failure to address both sides of the equation, or worse a demoralizing outcome for the people manager, creates distrust, drives up turnover, gives SPM a bad rap and the company a bad name.

Dealing with this derailer calls for:

- Understanding where the fear of developing successors comes from.

- Building a strong track record of rewarding people managers who develop future leaders.

- Engaging people managers in development planning for themselves resulting in their confidence in SPM.

- Educating people managers on the reality that their own career advancement may be stunted or rewards forfeited for failing to develop potential successors.

- Speaking directly about missed opportunities and risks to the promising performers, people managers, the department and the organization given the absence of SPM.

Derailer 4: SPM Induces Territorialism

Territorialism occurs when people managers resist releasing their employees to take on new opportunities outside their area of responsibility in the organization. The most common reasons for not wanting to part with their most promising performers include:

- Performance and productivity for which the manager is responsible may take a hit and so might their rewards.

- The promising performer's successor is not ready to take the reins or worse has not been identified.

- The promising performer was the only people manager's successor; so the people manager's timeline for advancement may get delayed.

Dealing with this derailer calls for:

- Reminding the people manager of his/her responsibilities for preparing employees for future needs of the organization and how results impact performance rating and compensation.

- Highlighting the benefits of the domino effect where one person's departure could create a wonderful development opportunity for another, and so on, and so on, and so on.

- Stressing the importance of distributing promising performers across the organization.

The vice president of corporate development at a $650M global company encountered this situation not all that long ago. One of his promising performers sought out a newly opened position as an opportunity for advancement. The vice president, let's call him Tom, engaged the employee, Sam, in a career discussion. During that conversation Tom sought to understand why Sam saw the new position as a stepping stone and revisit Sam's strengths and the kinds of work he most enjoys. Then the two compared requirements of the new position, in addition to other advancement alternatives, to Sam's strengths. Overall, Tom wanted to make sure Sam was making a good move for himself and for the company. Sam accepted the new position and provided Tom input on potential successors for his role along with ideas for mitigating risk for each candidate.

Our Vice President Tom later encountered a situation where an employee was readying himself for a new role but didn't possess every skill initially called for. Tom got creative and made sure that this promising performer had team members with complementary skills so collectively they covered all the bases. Further, Tom set the stage so each team member understood the unique skills he/she brought to the table. The solution worked very effectively.

Derailer 5: SPM Increases Unwanted Turnover

SPM is about preparing your future leaders. Many organizations are shaped like pyramids so there are fewer jobs as you navigate closer to the top. People managers worry that raising the hopes of promising performers who never realize their vertical advancement goals, or don't realize them soon enough, will result in increased unwanted turnover among the brightest.

Dealing with this derailer calls for:

- Acknowledging that yes, there is risk that promising performers in whom you invest will leave.

- Recognizing employee development is a critical retention tool. If your organization does not develop people, be aware that other employers do, which dramatically increases your chances of unwanted turnover.

- Expanding your "development" and "career enhancement and advancement" definitions to include:

  o Expanded scope within current responsibilities

- o Broadened range of experiences: stretch assignments and cross-functional projects with increased responsibility, risk and visibility

- o Job changes – promotions (vertical focus), transfers (horizontal focus), job rotations (example: expatriate assignments)

- Leaving room for the possibility that employees who leave your employ and later return will have broader and richer experiences from which your organization can benefit.

Consider Ken Margossian's experience. Ken is a knowledgeable executive, having worked in a number of mid-sized firms employing several hundred employees as well as large organizations with 20,000-plus employees over the course of his full career. Early on, with a lot of hard work, smarts, skills, and motivation he was successfully groomed for bigger leadership roles. Today, as a senior executive officer of a middle-market third generation family-owned business, Ken sets the stage for successful SPM. He's instrumental in designing and implementing SPM with his Human Resources partner. He shared an interesting story with me about SPM and turnover during our lunch interview.

Ken's firm hired a very talented, high energy sales manager who was quickly recognized as someone who would make major contributions in no time and had the bandwidth to take on the top sales and business development job. The firm did all the right things. It created, funded and supported a development plan to groom the fast tracker for the executive role. No challenge was too great for him to take on. Then one day out of the blue, he resigned. The entire executive team was floored. The management of this third generation family-owned business took the news very personally. So personally that it remains to be seen if the fast tracker would ever be welcomed back. Maybe time will heal that wound, maybe not. Ken went onto say that investing in employees is the right thing to do even though there are no guarantees.

Has your organization ever benefited from the Boomerang Effect? The Boomerang Effect essentially involves re-hiring past employees. Ipswitch, Nitsch Engineering, and the MOS have had enough positive experiences re-hiring former employees that they have shifted their attitude and actions. Yes, hiring former employees can be risky for a variety of reasons. However, the company can benefit from the new skills, experience, expertise, and broader range of contexts in which the former employees learned to operate while employed elsewhere. Further, given their previous tenure these folks know the company culture and expectations. While this mind shift is influencing re-hiring practices at increasingly more organizations, the terms under which each employee left and ability to navigate within the organization will also come into play when hiring decisions are made.

Derailer 6: SPM Ignites Jealousy

Jealousy can grow among participants in SPM and between participants and non-participants. Even employees who temporarily opt out of SPM for personal reasons can get wrapped up in bouts of jealousy.

Ken Margossian's company hired a sharp, fast track employee. This gentleman produced great results and had tremendous potential for advancement. He had the mix of skills, intelligence, results orientation and motivation not always seen in less experienced professionals. Over the time he was with the firm, it became obvious to his peers that he was being prepared for a larger role. He was frequently assigned special projects, attended executive and cross-functional meetings for increased exposure and shadowed executives to learn more about the inner operations of the business. It was not long before jealousy ensued among his co-workers which could not be ignored.

As a result, when rolling out SPM, Ken makes sure people managers are prepared for dealing with jealousy. Jealousy is an emotion that may involve negative thoughts and feelings of insecurity, distrust, fear, or anxiety over the loss of something. In the workplace the triggering event might be the co-worker who was invited to an executive meeting, who earned a higher pay increase or promotion, or who received recognition that another employee thought he/she deserved. The resulting behavior can tend to be power oriented like one-upmanship, trying to escalate one's stature by making others look bad or outright sabotage designed to prevent the newly promoted from being successful.

Ken advises people managers to observe jealous actions and the reactions of the promising potentials to whom they are directed. The ways people choose to behave says an awful lot. Their behaviors may be indicative of low, medium or high levels of emotional maturity. This kind of assessment, for starters, plays into development planning and coaching of both SPM participants and non-participants. Ken has found that employees respond extremely well to candid feedback and coaching. It can often be what lights a fire and inspires them to get onto the path of becoming a promising performer.

Dealing with this derailer calls for:

- Developing all employees; don't limit development to SPM participants.

- Recognizing that jealousy may grow to some degree among employees.

- Preparing people managers to effectively deal with jealousy.

- Coaching employees that participating in or permitting jealous behaviors detracts from career goal achievement.

- Making the tough call if repetitive bouts of jealousy make the person or others ineffective.

- Making some of the triggers of SPM related jealousy, such as getting executive visibility, available to non-participants too. It may be the spark that ignites the drive of a future leader.

Derailer 7: SPM Advances Only One Employee Segment

Is there a perception that only the new hires benefit from career advancement? Or is there a perception that longer service employees with strong relationships with executives benefit most from SPM? Your task then, is to analyze the data. What does it tell you? Is there any truth to the perception and if so, why? You may discover a bias that new hires are more favorably viewed due to their fresh ideas, different experiences, broader networks and independence from organizational politics. Or, conversely, you may find that long-service employees are viewed as dedicated contributors in good times and in bad, possess much needed institutional knowledge, and are capable of navigating within the organization, its culture and politics.

Dealing with this derailer calls for:

- Getting to the bottom of the perception and determining if it has merit.

- Taking action to correct the imbalance such as: encouraging and incentivizing long-service employees to take responsibility for scouting out new ideas and staying on top of best practices in their field so as not to lose their edge. Or encouraging executives to get better acquainted with the expertise and accomplishments of new hires.

Derailer 8: SPM Prompts More People Problems

People managers may encounter other challenges like employees not in agreement with the fields or areas in which you see them excelling in most or employees transferred or promoted among their peers. Let's explore a couple of examples.

Imagine that in the process of preparing an employee for greater responsibility you pushed him so far out of his comfort zone that he decided to leave the organization. Lisa Brothers of Nitsch Engineering recalls that exact scenario. As a general practice Lisa works with employees to match their strengths, interests and passions with stretch assignments that build confidence and serve as preparation for more responsibility. Occasionally, employees get tunnel vision and narrow the field of career advancement possibilities. A great people manager will test those boundaries, especially if they see potential not yet recognized by the employee. Long story short, this employee sought Lisa out years later to thank her for pushing him. It turns out that his career has advanced and he is doing the very type of work Lisa had been pushing him toward. A similar story rings true for another of Lisa's employees. She pushed this gentleman outside his comfort zone (which included completing course work, coaching and direct feedback including a 360° assessment). Today that employee has successfully expanded the scope of his job and is not even close to plateauing. To boot, his outlook on career possibilities widened dramatically.

Let's walk through another complexity. Transferring someone from their current department into another may seem to have low risk. But it could pose a unique set of issues not obvious from the get go. You see, each of us develops our own network of relationships in the course of doing our jobs. Think of this map as the informal organizational chart displaying our work relationships. Graphically mapping relationships shows that some employees have connections that look as if they are the center of spokes on a wheel. The relationship maps of others show them as one connection in a long narrow line of connections. And still others may have deep and broad reaching relationships that span vertically and horizontally throughout the entire organization. To add further complexity, the relationship map for any one person will vary depending upon the dimension used for mapping the relationships. So, a work connections map will differ from social, industry expertise, career advice and innovation relationship maps. While viewed as a bit invasive, relationship mapping is a management tool that is gaining momentum in SPM as well as other applications like mergers and acquisitions.

Let's get back to our employee transfer. Essentially, the employee is plucked out of his/her relationship map and dropped into another where he/she may have to start anew in building relationships. Some folks won't skip a beat in this situation while others will struggle. Either way advanced notice of this potential phenomenon and coaching can help get the employee back on track.

Promoting someone among their peers can be riskier than a transfer. These promising performers may need to build new relationships, improve their skills in dealing with jealousy, and strategize on managing the power structure.

Think back to Ken Rubin, the general manager who built the $350M+ Healthcare business where one third of the contributing employees are fully dedicated to his organization and the other two thirds are resources shared throughout Iron Mountain. Think about the importance of relationship building within that organization! Ken goes to great lengths in helping his folks build and navigate relationships within and outside the Healthcare business.

Dealing with this derailer calls for:

- Helping employees expand their self-imposed career interests by reflecting on many options.

- Recognizing the impact that employee relationship maps have on future assignments in addition to the speed at which they get acclimated to the new assignments.

HIGHLIGHTS

- Understand, educate, and mitigate potential derailers of SPM before they occur.

- Use change management practices suitable for your organization when implementing SPM. This is especially true among organizations implementing SPM for the first time and those that have tried unsuccessfully in the past.

Chapter 7

Derailer 9: Career Conversations

This is the story of a $75M manufacturer of custom wire and cable, cable assemblies and coil cords serving the medical, industrial, military, data collection, multimedia, renewable energy, and data and telecommunications markets. The president, let's call him Frank, stepped into his new executive role following fifty years of leadership provided by the company's original founder followed by his son. And while the company has undergone several transformations as a family-owned business, the new owner – a private equity firm – has great expectations of the company.

Frank concedes that a succession plan would have been tremendously valuable when he took the helm. As the new business strategy evolves, a succession plan would have accelerated his getting acquainted with employees who possess critical knowledge, know-how and skills to sustain the current business.

There are three things you should know about Frank's starting point. First, most of the employees had not been engaged in what they perceived to be meaningful conversations about their job responsibilities or performance expectations – never mind the preparation needed to realize their career aspirations. Second, Frank needed to convince his executive team to shift their perspective and appreciate building company success through its people. Then he had to teach his team how. Third, Frank doesn't limit succession planning to leadership roles. He thinks far more broadly about the core competencies required to sustain the organization and position it for future success. As a result, employees who possess mission critical capabilities can and are identified regardless of level in the organization and include leaders as well as individual contributors.

While career conversations are ongoing at the manufacturing company, Frank's previous assignments resulted in significant turnaround in employee performance, development achievement and improved organizational results through SPM efforts that started with career conversations. His first piece of advice is being cognizant of your starting point. Past voids on people performance, expectations, and development is no reason to dismiss employees from the SPM. For many, all it takes is one meaningful and authentic career conversation to light a fire — a critical step in the SPM data collection process.

Paul Fontaine, now the Vice President of Education at the MOS, was engaged in periodic career conversations by several executives early on in his career. At the time of these conversations Paul's position was roughly two to three levels below those of the executives. He remembers these "skip level conversations" fondly, and emphasizes that they helped him crystallize his career plan. Moreover, the conversations motivated him forward. The executive sponsors supported him throughout his journey through career conversations, coaching, feedback, and resources which played a role in preparing Paul for larger responsibilities, new assignments, and eventually promotions.

Today, Paul puts his positive experience to work at the MOS. Naturally, employees who report to him directly have first-hand experience with career conversations and the resulting development planning, feedback, and coaching. They understand the flow of the conversations as well as how thought provoking and motivational they can be.

Paul educates people managers as a group on the purpose, goals and approaches to preparing employees for larger or different responsibilities. He contextualizes their efforts: "We have a responsibility to employees as well as the community at large to sustain the institution for generations to come." He finds that transparency during skip level conversations greatly reduces the risk of people managers perceiving SPM as a job security threat (see Chapter 6, Derailer 3). Paul prepares the managers for the conversations by mapping out topics to be covered, when to redirect employees back to their direct managers, anticipating tough questions employees may pose, and action planning. The people managers are not only encouraged but expected to conduct skip level conversations with their employees. The managers find the exchanges valuable when leveraging talent across the organization. Plus it increases their comfort level when Paul has skip level conversations with their folks.

Paul is an absolute believer in skip level conversations as they can essentially result in better SPM and create sponsorship like roles among executives in the organization. He offers this pearl of wisdom: be thoughtful on expectations set with the employee and who owns the next steps.

For instance, Paul recalls a gentleman who was thrilled to be engaged by Paul in a career conversation – especially given the levels of separation between them. He was enthusiastic and toward the end of their discussion Paul said something along the lines of "Keep me posted." The gentleman took this literally; so, Paul began receiving a flurry of daily updates on his progress. The lesson learned: be clear on who owns the action item of coaching and monitoring progress.

Think career conversations serve only long-term goals of SPM? Not so, they can have immediate benefits too. I was working with a group of executives on their initial roll-out of SPM. Each executive engaged their employees in career conversations as preparation for their first talent review intended to broaden employee visibility among the executives. Before starting to facilitate the session, one of the executives, with great exuberance, shared his recent experience with the career conversations. Unbeknownst to this executive, let's call him Steve, one of his employees was a day away from resigning. About half way through the career conversation, the employee, let's call him Roger, disclosed his plans to accept a job offer. However, Roger ultimately decided to turn it down. Why? Because he liked his co-workers and boss, was enthusiastic about current and future products and enjoyed his job.

What had driven Roger to consider other job offers? His current job had one missing piece: the opportunity to develop and grow professionally. Because Roger felt the company would support his growth, he elected to stay. Today, Roger is one of the most highly motivated learners. All the executives were taken back by this experience. It was a wonderful segue into the talent review.

Career conversations are analogous to strategic planning conversations. Without them, it's easy for people to get lost in performing lots of seemingly important and unimportant related activities without benefit of context like direction, goals, external forces, feedback, and clarity on successful outcomes. When it goes on for too long, people feel like they are on a hamster's running wheel, running as fast as they can on the road to nowhere. And that is the quickest way to prompt a brain drain when the job market strengthens and promising performers choose to hop off the running wheel. Get over it. Career development is part of your responsibilities as people manager. And we already know that failing to develop employees fuels unwanted turnover.

A lot happens during these conversations: aligning employee passion and interests with business needs, increasing employee satisfaction and engagement, improving employee retention, and strengthening trust. Further, when done in context, such as succession planning, career conversations and the resulting action plans help people managers leverage talent across the organization to improve organizational productivity, performance and profitability. This kind of forward thinking about human capital is an integral part of business planning and risk management.

What's the next hurdle people managers must get over? Fear. Fear of not having the answers to all the tough questions posed by employees. The highly volatile economic times in which we live have undoubtedly contributed to this fear. What can or should you say? How can you support career aspirations without making guarantees? What about the worry of squashing aspirations? What if that next level job is not available when your employee is ready? What if your employee is ready but a co-worker or new hire is awarded the position? If these are some of your concerns then that is a good sign!

A helpful solution involves creating a list of frequently asked questions you'll likely encounter from employees during career conversations. Include the toughest questions – after all, the most promising performers won't hold back. Jointly discuss the questions with peer people managers and Human Resources; their perspectives will help shape a thoughtful response. Keep in mind that questions concerning job security issues require frank answers and not sugar coated responses. Even when you are prepared, you may still get questions for which you don't have answers. A simple "I don't know" will suffice. Respond truthfully and come up with a plan for how you and the employee navigate to an answer. The career conversation is instrumental in strengthening trust between you and the employee so there is no room for inauthentic dialogue. Just be frank. I often find it helps to stress that the quickest way to miss out on a career growth opportunity is to fail to prepare for it in advance.

Jump Starting Career Conversations

Start small with the one-on-one conversation. Focus on a recent experience prompting the employee to reflect on how things went and their key takeaways. It could be as simple as asking:

- *"How do you think it went?"*
  That kind of interaction can segue into broader conversation about strengths, development areas as well as career aspirations. Simply ask the employee to *"Give it more thought as to how it fits into your career aspirations then let's get together next week to talk it through."*

Using a comprehensive approach to career conversations is more common when rolling-out a new SPM program – especially for the first time and for employees with whom you have not worked long. The following guidelines focus on the type of work that energizes the employee while supporting and encouraging the employee to take ownership for career building activities:

- Understand the types of work the employee is most proud of.
  "Tell me about three experiences over the course of your career that you are most proud of and enjoyed the most."

- Do a deeper dive to understand why the
  employee's experience was so remarkable.
  Understanding what energizes the employee
  can't be underestimated. Its value could grow
  exponentially if it spills over onto co-workers too.
  *"What was it about this experience that made it
  so remarkable?"*

Jointly explore the work and its characteristics. Identify what the employee found most challenging (technical issues, people issues, timeline, resources, etc.). Distinguish the employee's work from his or her coworkers: pace of work, management style, culture, results generated and how success was measured, what the employee learned and would do next time if assigned similar work.

- Identify the skills and knowledge associated with
  the work.
  *"What skills, knowledge and know-how are
  critical to success in doing the kind of work you
  enjoy so much? Of those, which do you feel are
  your strengths – and which could benefit from
  more practice?"*

- Explore and identify new or like experiential work
  assignments that serve both an organizational need
  and help the employee grow.
  *"What projects or work do you see in our
  organization that are of greatest interest given
  the kind of work you enjoy most and skills you'd
  like to further develop?"*

- Connect the experiential work assignment with the employee's desired career future.
  "How does doing progressively more complex work of this type fit into your desired career path? Looking forward, what responsibilities, jobs or career paths do you most desire? How else could you prepare? Which career paths have you decided against and why?"

Explore other areas that may be of relevance to potential work assignments, such as interest and ability to travel or relocate, etc.

- Create an action plan that accounts for: goals and defining what success looks like, specific preparation work, experiential work assignments, the approach and frequency of feedback, and measuring results.

- Follow up on the action plan.

This above approach builds trust and its implementation builds employee confidence in addition to capabilities needed most in the organization.

Time Saver: Assign writing the development plan to the employee; it serves as one indicator of the employee's true motivation level.

Of course, the actual career conversations may take twists and turns not mapped out above. So, just like you anticipated the tough career questions, do what you can to prepare. Anticipate surprises like: the employee wants to pursue responsibilities that do not play to his strengths, the employee limits career advancement to vertical promotions thereby ruling out horizontal career moves, the employee's timeline for career advancement is unrealistic, or the organization is not able to provide the kind of work of greatest interest to the employee. Conversely, you might discover that the employee seeks only to expand her current set of responsibilities, which may be easily managed.

HIGHLIGHTS

- As the new leader do not assume roles, responsibilities, and expectations have been clarified with employees for their current roles let alone roles and responsibilities they may aspire to.

- Educate people managers on how to navigate career conversations and expected outcomes. There is nothing like first-hand experience as a teacher.

- Leverage talent across the organization to improve organizational productivity, performance and profitability through career conversations.

- Reap the many benefits of career conversations: align employee passion and interests with business needs, increase employee satisfaction and engagement, improve employee retention, and strengthen trust.

Chapter 8
Talent Magnet Tool Kit

Many executives interviewed disclosed that day-to-day operations are nearly all-consuming, resulting in insufficient time and resources dedicated to SPM – particularly as it relates to thoughtfully preparing employees for different responsibilities. Remember, preparation work or development is at the heart of SPM. And study after study shows that employee development and engagement are tightly related to employee retention and organizational performance.

Preparing employees for different responsibilities need not be time-consuming. A development plan (the product of career conversations) is an efficient way to capture career enhancement and advancement goals and preparation commitments. From a practical standpoint a plan is not a plan until it has been written down: a responsibility easily delegated to employees and completed by those serious about their own development.

When pulling together a development plan, the General Manager of a European-based division within a large global healthcare company, let's call her Jan, stresses the importance of matching ambition and desires of the employee with business need. Jan coaches her direct reports to identify not one, but several career growth strategies as well as their respective skills gaps. This can prevent employees from latching onto just one venue for career growth, which may prove to be disappointing. Considering several career growth strategies opens people's minds to the practical application of transferrable skills and provides the organization more options as it builds bench strength and redeploys people.

Sustainable learning starts with development planning and includes approaches that:

- Clarify expectations of targeted responsibilities and relevant skills, etc.

- Create employee awareness as to their starting point along the learning curve.

- Provide cognitive understanding of what they commit to learn.

- Foster experiential learning in a safe environment.

- Provide on the job opportunities to put the new skills and insights to work.

The remainder of this chapter outlines a myriad of people preparation and development venues. Open your mind to the possibilities then narrow down the list. Select the venues that best fit your organization, its culture, its pocketbook, and the learning styles of your future leaders.

Assessments

Assessments are an insightful and objective way for increased understanding of employees, their strengths and development areas of in-demand skills, performance, and future potential. Depending upon the type, before and after assessments are of great value so that employees can gauge progress made on development efforts. Listing all the different types of assessments and how to correctly apply them is beyond the scope of this book. Suffice it to say that using several assessments is preferable to relying on just one. It is analogous to using multiple screening techniques in the recruiting process to gather relevant views of candidates rather than relying on one form of assessment such as the resume paper screen for example.

The leadership profile is a basis for assessment and a tool frequently used in SPM. Why? Because the profile itself captures the leadership attributes, behaviors, knowledge, know-how and skills (i.e. competencies or capabilities) your organization needs of its leaders. When used for assessing talent each employee gains an understanding of individual strengths and areas that warrant improvement. Further the results can drive learning solutions such as training for groups of people with common development needs as well as individual learning needs that may warrant a personalized solution such as coaching. The leadership profile is one of the first design elements I use when collaborating with clients on SPM.

Iron Mountain, for instance, created a leadership profile for its general management executive role. The profile consists of seven categories and subcategories of competencies, all of which define how successful general managers operate and behave. The profile is used as an assessment tool to gauge preparation work for future general managers. Iron Mountain has developed profiles for other job families as well. The competencies within a job family vary by level; for example, what's expected of vice presidents differs from expectations of middle managers.

Delegate

Delegating work to others helps employees prepare for different responsibilities and frees you up to take on new work assignments too. It is low cost, win-win and one of the most effective ways to elevate performance across the entire organization!

New Job Responsibility

Enhancing or adding new job responsibilities typically includes assignments that are of higher level, more complex, require the application of new skills or differ in some way from existing responsibilities. These characteristics may also apply to cross-functional projects and high visibility assignments.

According to Azonix's past President, Greg Baletsa, Azonix made the application of learning and development a priority and set that expectation not just with leaders but with employees through its Greatness, Proficiency and Agility Program (GPA). Greatness stood for the exceptional work and contribution of employees, proficiency had to do with learning and efficiently applying the new skills on the job, and agility was about being a flexible asset to the business. GPA instilled the development imperative among employees so much so that if managers were not proactive then employees would call them on it. Here is how it worked. Each year Azonix executives selected a few areas of learning most needed in the organization. Past examples include: lean, problem solving, and team development. Employees were urged to develop the skills not just through learning forums facilitated by the company but through their application on the job. The GPA program drove employees to their managers to identify work assignments for applying the new skills. You see, the opportunity to earn recognition and reward were contingent upon applying the new skills to the job. And what did employees get for applying the new skills? They earned recognition at both monthly all-hands meetings as well as the public display of GPAs earned by every employee. They also had the opportunity to earn quarterly and annual bonuses. GPA was instrumental in both individual and organizational development.

Steve Petter, a global supply chain management executive, shared the story of a professional, let's call him Rob, who had his sights on advancing in the electrical engineering arena. Rob really got a kick out of solving business problems through the engagement of people – and he was good at it too. Through career conversations Rob disclosed to Steve his apprehension about abandoning the technical track for the people leadership track. After a frank conversation that his technical skills were not quite as strong as his people and business problem solving skills, Rob agreed to move into the new role. The role had fewer technical responsibilities but far greater people responsibilities thus the leadership and problem solving opportunities were infinite. Now Rob soars in his new role despite his initial reservations.

Sponsored Special Assignments

When I am working with clients, one of the SPM goals is to ensure that many executives get familiar with a wider range of employees and their contributions and capabilities. That is because choosing a successor for a pivotal role requires the endorsement and support of several and not just one executive. Each executive must have established a level of trust that the successor has what it takes to effectively perform the job. Thus, when assigning special projects, I advocate the assignment of a sponsor as well. The sponsor is not the employee's direct manager. The sponsor takes an active coaching role and employees appreciate the new perspectives. Given enough assignments with different sponsors, many executives will have the familiarity needed when it comes time to make deployment decisions.

A $100M+ medical devices firm that has grown rapidly makes use of special change projects assigned to groups made up of a cross-functional SPM participants. The projects are business challenges that must be addressed. The groups work together over the course of several months to analyze the problem and come up with solutions that specifically address quality, recognition, innovation and change management issues. So not only do business problems get solved but the team members learn to work together, they engage in 2-way conversations with executives and present final recommendations. This connects the employees to the day-to-day issues that executives face and certainly strengthens employee engagement levels.

Cross-Functional Projects

Cross-functional projects are commonplace since most organizations have core business processes that cut across functions which must be executed in a repeatable, efficient, and error-free way. When it comes to SPM, cross-functional project teams take on a whole new meaning. That is because in SPM, when done well, leaders are developed one-by-one *and* as a team.

Let's say you expect four of eight executives to retire within a few years of each other. Each executive diligently develops likely successors. The executives retire and their successors assume the new positions as planned. It is not long before you realize that the mix of new executives does not work; they are not gelling together as a team – or worse, they are at each other's throats and failing to get anything done. Lesser things have put new executives out on the street. Bottom line: develop future leaders individually and in teams with other likely future leaders to make sure all play well together. Cross-functional teams are ideal for this purpose.

The MOS has a track record of establishing cross-functional teams to plan and manage large exhibitions that come to town. These projects are perfect for preparing promising performers at all levels of the organization for future assignments, giving them broad, cross-divisional museum experience and enhancing effectiveness in their current roles. The projects require employees to influence and collaborate with one another, and in some cases leading sub-teams of employees from different departments. Employees find the experiences valuable because they stretch their capabilities, grow their networks, and deepen relationships. Visibility of contributing employees is expanded among a broader range of executives. Executives appreciate the early insight on who may be having difficulty long before being placed in a larger or different role. Executives and project managers coach and work with the employees more closely to overcome challenges.

As part of preparing future leaders of KLR to take the reins, about four years ago an executive committee of four people was formed. Formerly all strategic and operational decisions for the firm were made by the two founders. Today the executive committee has input on all decisions. The committee's early days were instrumental in elevating the strategic thinking skills of committee members. In recent years, the executive committee has formalized into a governing body addressing daily issues. It reports results to the shareholders quarterly, and shareholder agreements reflect their larger role in running the organization. In order to help shape the strategic direction of the firm the executive committee has formed a "futures committee" to get feedback on determining future strategy. Its membership includes all current shareholders, all members of the Emerging Leaders Academy (to be described to you soon) as well as some lesser experienced influential employees of the firm.

Debriefings

Couple debriefings with new job responsibilities, sponsored special assignments, and cross-functional projects to reinforce and accelerate learning. Integrate debriefings with coaching, mentoring and job shadowing too! Refer back to Chapter 5 and the "1 - 2 - 3 Debriefing" for the how tos.

Coaching

Coaching equips people with the right environment, tools, feedback, opportunity to reflect, and action plan for increased effectiveness on the job. Coaching typically extends over a period of time with a focus on: solutions not problems, self-discovery, commitment to action, and accountability for achieving goals.

Coaching can be provided on a real-time basis by direct managers and project managers during the course of the normal workday. Or, it can be formal personified by scheduled coaching sessions with an internal or external coach.

Coaching is used in a range of contexts including but not limited to: to reinforce employee use of concepts, tools and techniques covered in workshops; help an employee become more effective in a current role; help an employee prepare for a new role; and help a new team member assimilate into an existing team or organization's culture. Who could forget the favorable impact coaching had on Jay Leader (Chapter 3) shortly following his near-death experience?

Mentoring

Mentoring is a learning venue that differs from coaching in that the mentor in the relationship typically has first-hand experience that is of keen interest to the mentee. While a mentoring relationship can be goal and accountability oriented like coaching, it is often consumed with conversation where the mentor imparts wisdom by sharing historical experiences, highlighting situational factors, and even advising the mentee on how to proceed.

The demand for reciprocal mentoring is growing. An example lies at the intersection of the generations where Generation Y mentors the older generations on technology, for example, and in turn Baby Boomers mentor Generation Y on non-technical aspects of work and business.

Mentoring groups are growing in popularity too, such as the mentoring circles of the Healthcare Business Women's Association Boston Chapter. As one of two mentors I had the pleasure to take part in a mentoring circle consisting of four mentees in senior leadership positions of life science organizations. The mentees drive the topics covered, and after a couple of sessions, take ownership for agenda setting and leading the sessions. Learning is abundant among mentees and mentors alike.

Priscilla Geigis, the Director of Division of State Parks and Recreation, introduced the Park Fellows Program to the Massachusetts Department of Conservation and Recreation. The goal of the program was to fill the pipeline with the next generation of full-time park professionals. Given the shoestring budget, creating the program had its challenges. Training, individual and group experiential work assignments, and a strong mentoring program were its primary components. Participants with experienced, attentive mentors got the most out of the program. Mentors walked away more energized than ever. While the actual number of full-time park professional new hires was lower than anticipated, due to dramatic budget challenges, some group special assignments resulted in lasting legacies such as a recycling program, yoga on the Esplanade, and the plan for a disc golf program (where Frisbees are thrown into metal baskets affixed to poles, sounds like fun!). Priscilla is ready to roll again with the program when the timing is right because it produced so many fine results.

Job Shadowing

Job shadowing is a way to learn by seeing someone in action rather than reading a job description or being told how to perform the responsibilities. Because the person is seen in action the learner also picks up on nuances, the context and situational factors that shine through after several job shadowing experiences.

Carrie Hammond, the new Chief Executive Officer of the Hartford Symphony Orchestra (HSO) a non-profit organization, takes shadowing to the next level. She encourages her direct reports to shadow their counterparts in larger organizations. Carrie's robust network makes shadowing easy to orchestrate and it is relatively inexpensive too.

Similarly the MOS reaps the rewards of shadowing. For example, an employee traveled to a science museum in France to shadow an admirable leader making great strides in an area of interest to the MOS. The employee benefited not just in his own development but the organization benefited too by better understanding the underpinnings and success factors of implementing innovative approaches.

Workshops

Nearly all the companies I spoke with at some point or another make use of workshops to address learning needs common to a group of employees. Workshops are a cost-effective and efficient way to reinforce expectations, establish a common language and approach, provide cognitive understanding on the topic, and offer a safe environment for experiential learning. It's not uncommon for assessments, games, and simulations to be integrated into workshops to maximize effectiveness.

The Emerging Leaders Academy at KLR, a $35M accounting firm and winner of numerous professional awards was recently launched. Larry Kahn, founder and CEO of KLR, described the program to me over a cup of coffee. Essentially the program is designed to prepare the accounting firm's third generation of future leaders through a three year commitment to: participate in monthly seminars and follow-on coaching, complete an annual special project, attend a national management conference of accounting firms, participate in quarterly dinner meetings featuring New England speakers, and mentoring. Of course, the content of the Academy's sessions is of great value since it directly supports the development of core capabilities KLR needs of its future leaders. Just as important as the content is the relationship building that occurs among the nine employees who get to complete the program together. While the leadership needs of KLR are unique and reflected in the Academy's design, partnering with other organizations for content delivery has tremendously expanded their capabilities.

MOS adds a twist when it comes to leadership development workshops. Their initial leadership training was customized by a few MOS executives including Paul Fontaine, Jonathan Burke, Britton O'Brien (the Vice President of Human Resources), and a learning and development professional. The executives participated in the workshops and completed the training curriculum. A small group of executives participated in a train-the-trainer workshop and were paired to deliver the same training to the next level of supervisors, not just their direct reports. The cost effective and sustainable program was designed to be museum specific and create a common language around leadership. MOS has experienced great value in re-inforcing leadership lessons using this cascade approach.

Peer Learning Forums

Peer learning forums are sessions where colleagues with common interests share knowledge and experience with one another and ask tough questions of each other intended to help peers move closer to the achievement of a challenging goal. The forums serve as a vehicle to (1) set goals, (2) share experiences, information and advice, (3) involve two way communications, and (4) recognize that each peer participant will be a learner one minute and an advisor the next. And because the forums are participant-driven they can occur as a one-time exchange or extend over a period of time. The forums are growing in prevalence inside organizations where participation is limited to employees, where a "book club" model may be used, and outside organizations such as those orchestrated by professional associations and the like. The latter has gained momentum especially when peer participants come from non-competing organizations and essentially operate as each other's advisors.

Relationship Building

Building and sustaining relationships often becomes more important than subject matter expertise as one's career advances – particularly for people advancing to the executive ranks. Back in Chapter 3 we touched on relationship maps, the different dimensions of relationships that can be mapped, the types of connectors, and the fact that plucking someone out of one relationship map and dropping them into another may be more challenging than anticipated. The act of mapping relationships while still in its infancy can be insightful when supporting an employee's acclimation to a new group.

Professional Association & Trade
Group Membership and Participation

While each association and trade group has its own value proposition, most include: content to keep you updated on best practices and recent developments, the potential to earn continuing education units, visible commitment to your profession or your industry via membership, opportunities to expand your network, volunteer opportunities to deepen relationships, resources, and a membership directory when you need access to experts. This one-stop shopping may satisfy a variety of development needs.

Volunteerism

People volunteer for causes they feel strongly about and the desire to have impact. Motivation like that can promote stepping outside of one's comfort zone. That's why volunteerism can also provide on-the-job training with an organization other than your own. Keep an eye and ear open to learn where employees volunteer and the results they generate. It may just prompt you to encourage their continued volunteerism not only to contribute to the cause they care about but as part of preparing for stretch assignments in the workplace.

For example, imagine that a technician on a manufacturing floor repeatedly threw his hat into the ring for a supervisory job. While he got turned down twice because he did not possess the required leadership skills, he did not give up on his dream. Since his employer provided no formal leadership training he found an alternative that married his favorite past time, hiking, with opportunity to practice newly acquired leadership skills. He attended a two-day leadership workshop provided by his hiking club and then volunteered to lead hikes. Over the next year or so he led many hikes, very much enjoying each one. The next time a supervisory job opened he applied for it and got it! His newly acquired leadership skills were spilling out onto the production floor and that made him the ideal candidate for the job.

Volunteerism paved Carrie Hammond's way to her most enjoyable executive role as the CEO of the HSO. Carrie is the daughter of a musician, her mother, and a corporate executive, her father. Early on in her career, Travelers Insurance supported her in a number of ways: participation in a highly sought after job rotation program, a volunteer opportunity with the HSO through its corporate responsibility program, and completion of Harvard Business School's two-year program. Interestingly enough, Carrie provided several letters of recommendation to get into Harvard including one from her volunteer work with the Executive Director at HSO. After managing a profit and loss center for the Power Systems Spare Parts Group of Pratt & Whitney and working a part-time stent when her children were young, Carrie took a full-time role managing corporate responsibility programs at United Technologies Corporation (UTC), Pratt's parent company. That role provided opportunity to assess and distribute corporate funds to arts organizations around the world, including the HSO. While budget cuts resulted in the elimination of the corporate responsibility jobs at UTC, it turned out to be a magnificent stroke of luck. It was not long before Carrie was recruited to become the CEO of HSO.

Authorship, Speaking & Presenting

The value of authorship, speaking and presenting is multi-faceted. The employee becomes known as the resident expert and the go-to person in his or her field. Writing and speaking skills are enhanced. Personal brand is enriched. Because authoring, speaking, and presenting also have the potential to contribute to the organization's brand any of these could easily become a sponsored special assignment.

The $75M manufacturing company referenced earlier makes use of internal speaking opportunities as a way for promising performers to gain visibility and credibility with executives as well as the board of directors. In this venue it is often the president who takes on the sponsor role. Development may take the form of objective setting, reviewing presentation materials, practicing delivery, or anticipating questions posed by the executives followed by debriefing.

Coursework

Coursework at colleges, universities, or other institutes be it for continuing education, to earn a degree or certificate can be instrumental in employees learning a body of knowledge or specific discipline to facilitate career advancement and changes. Examples include the technician looking to advance into engineering, the senior engineer seeking a product marketing management role, and so on. This venue is largely focused on providing cognitive understanding of the topic.

Reading

Reading is vastly underestimated and can foster kernels of breakthrough and innovative thinking. It is also a key component to many of the other learning venues. Reading's easy on the budget and easy to build into anyone's schedule. Sifting through the masses of the written word is a skill well worth developing.

Knowledge Management

Capture intellectual capital while developing folks. By this I mean capture the knowledge in a useful way that also preserves organizational memory. One of the simplest ways to accomplish this is to ask employees to document and/or record (i.e. audio, visual or other) what they know and have learned. Then store and refer to it as needed. Documenting reinforces employee lessons and storing preserves institutional recall that has the potential to extend the knowledge to others.

HIGHLIGHTS

- Prepare employees for different responsibilities; it is at the heart of SPM.

- Delegate to develop and free up your time. It's a win-win.

- Tap into a wide range of preparation venues to fit individual needs and the organizational wallet.

- Prioritize the most effective forms of employee development: experiential work assignments for practicing and mastering new skills, on-going coaching, mentoring, and debriefings.

- Commit a percent of your time to SPM and build it into your schedule just like any other business priority.

Chapter 9

Wanted: Blue Boxers

There is an interesting interdependency that exists between hiring from the internal and external talent pools. The advantages from the internal talent pool include: the organization's deep familiarity with the employee's performance, potential, accomplishments, passion, resilience, style, strengths, and blind spots. Additionally, promising performers will have demonstrated mastery at working effectively within the organization's culture and navigating the organization by having built a strong network. Consistent with messages of this book, internal hiring favorably impacts engagement, retention and organizational performance. All these factors increase the chances of the internal candidate's success in the new position.

On the other hand, the pros of the external talent pool include: fresh perspectives and approaches that could favorably impact growth, productivity and profitability as well as increases in industry experience, specialized knowledge, or skills needed by the organization. We have all lived through both scenarios and could elaborate on more pros and cons associated with each.

To embellish the nuances and interdependencies between internal and external hiring, I share with you the story of Paul Kirwin, President & Chief Executive Officer of Northcott Hospitality.

After years of leadership experience working in hospitality and lodging big brands like Hyatt, Regent and Radisson, Paul joined Northcott (which is a $300M+ franchisor and operator of hotel and restaurant chains including: AmericInn® hotels and Houlihan's® and Perkins Restaurant & Bakery®). Northcott also provides design and build, procurement, and general contracting services through its services division.

Fifteen hundred employees strong, Paul and the Chairman partnered to put into place the company's first SPM that went beyond the planning of CEO successors. The targeted jobs include corporate management jobs and management jobs geographically dispersed among the company owned hotels and restaurants. The primary goals of SPM at Northcott were to (1) prepare potential replacement successors in the case of expected or unexpected job vacancies and (2) build leadership bench strength for the future. Year one of implementation started at the initiative of Paul and the Board of Directors, and focused on identifying and developing potential successors for executive jobs or those jobs that report directly to Paul. In the second year of implementation, SPM was expanded to include the remaining management positions.

The most useful tools in the SPM process in Paul's eyes include the 9 Box grid, where employee performance and potential are objectively assessed and calibrated across the organization, and the organizational chart which denotes potential successors for each mission critical position.

At Northcott the boxes in the organizational chart are color-coded to convey the estimated amount of time to prepare employees for future positions. The designations include: "ready now," "ready in one to two years," or "ready in three to five years." The boxes designated as "ready in one to two years" are color-coded blue. Why is that significant? Because when reviewing the organizational charts, an absence of employee entries in blue boxes raises a big red flag. The absence of "blue boxers" means that the company is at risk of having no potential successors from the internal candidate pool ready to take on new responsibilities in one to two years.

If a manager leaves and does not have any blue boxers, business operations are sure to be disrupted. At Northcott, rather than simply hope for the best, the company turns to the other part of the talent management equation, external hiring, to populate the blue boxes. The result? The hiring criterion used to assess external candidates is raised to blue boxer levels. The goal at Northcott is to have several blue boxers for each mission critical position and groom those employees so that the company has more options when filling key roles due to growth or job vacancy. Northcott's early successes reinforce the importance of this goal.

The net effect of this approach has elevated the importance of the external hiring process to Northcott. The hiring process has been revamped, assessments and other tools added, and managers better educated not to simply reduce the risk of hiring mistakes but to increase blue boxer hiring practices. This approach is more difficult than it sounds when putting into practice. The path of least resistance is to hire people who could perform responsibilities of the immediate job opening. Hiring blue boxer quality candidates takes more vigor and may lengthen the time to fill the job. Executives first need to walk the talk when hiring their own direct reports. And they must be vigilant in guiding others to do the same even if it means extending the length of a search until a blue boxer is hired.

Steve Petter, supply chain executive of a global technology firm, also stresses the importance of high potential external hiring and succession planning not just at the top level but at every level in the organization. After umpteen stories he told me over a cup of coffee it was clear a first line supervisor new hire may in fact be the first step toward hiring a future director or vice president. Thus, the thinking processes, attitudes, and past recruiting approaches need to change to benefit from blue boxer hiring.

It doesn't take long to recognize that George's background, the executive cited from Chapter 6's Derailer 3, is both deep and broad by design. Initially a mechanical engineer, George's career includes leadership roles in general management, mergers and acquisitions, business development, domestic and international sales, operations, and product development. He signed up as General Manager to turnaround a security company providing access cards, accompanying software, and electronics. The $35M revenue company had gotten into some trouble with federal regulators. The turnaround was challenging given George's goals to: grow the company, return it to a position of strong profitability, square away things with regulators, and groom his successor.

George inherited an eight person management team without benefit of a succession plan. His first job was to assess the members of his team using an objective albeit informal approach. Over the course of nine months changes to the management were made. Only the finance and sales executives stayed on. Operations, engineering, quality, marketing, etc. were replaced. George's approach to recruiting replacements was thoughtful and deliberate. He brought in people who had: strong functional expertise, a broad business background, and experience with significant responsibility and achievements for a function other than the one being hired for. He also looked for well educated, motivated, and ambitious candidates. Once hired, he augmented their existing backgrounds and experience with new on-the-job development experiences. Over time the team gained broader business skills under George's leadership. This "make and buy" approach helped George to get ahead of the curve in developing a successor for the general management job.

Development venues included special projects, expanded responsibilities within current job, job changes, and exposure to different ways of thinking through participation in forums and meetings that they would not have been included in otherwise. Occasionally people would push back. But during debriefs they realized the value of participating in the forums. And while the company did not have a formal SPM process,

George expected his direct reports to do their own planning and pay careful attention to whom they hired.

After several years, the parent company acquired other organizations, which resulted in George picking up additional responsibilities. When he left, the company had grown to $100M in revenue and the operations executive moved into the general manager role.

Advice? George believes the questions that must be asked and answered when assessing potential successors include:

- Can they do it? This gets to the issue of capability.

- Do they want to? This gets to the issue of motivation and passion.

- How long will it take to prepare someone for a new job or responsibility? This gets to the issue of practicality from the business perspective. If it takes too long to prepare someone and you must go outside, then be deliberate in your hiring practices (i.e. hire blue boxers).

Blue boxer external hiring can have a very favorable affect on existing employees. While employees at first may experience disappointment for missing out on new responsibilities awarded to new hires, it can also prompt them to take their own performance up a notch. You may see improved performance, increased initiative, staying current with relevant best practices, technologies, etc. among the internal candidate pool. People managers too may turn up the heat in terms of better preparing internal candidates so that they are better contenders for future job vacancies.

This was the case with a blue boxer high performing manager, let's call him Ralph, in the $75M manufacturing company managed by Frank, the new president. Ralph, one level below the senior leadership team, showed great promise. Frank purposely developed Ralph through a series of job rotations including quality, materials planning, and operations. Co-workers noticed and began inquiring about rotations for themselves. Frank indicated that employees quickly understood that he walked the talk when it came to employee development for the purposes of stimulating career growth and organizational performance.

Back at Northcott, each year Paul and the executives work through the SPM process. Once consolidated, Paul presents the snapshot along with key workforce analytics to the Board of Directors. Bringing SPM to the board level does several things. It elevates the importance of talent management as a form of risk management, creates visibility for high potential employees and prompts board oversight, engagement, and support in leadership development investments and decisions.

HIGHLIGHTS

- With laser-like focus, identify blue boxers (i.e. internal candidates "ready in one to two years" to fill mission critical positions).

- Recognize the importance of using blue boxer criteria in both internal and external hiring.

- Exercise vigilant leadership so that blue boxer hiring is not compromised by short-term thinking when hiring external candidates.

- Transparency when it comes to blue boxer external hiring will motivate internal candidates to step up their game for future career growth opportunities.

Chapter 10

The Board and Talent Analytics

Back in November of 2009 USA Today reported, "When Bank of America CEO Kenneth Lewis said that he was resigning, no one was surprised. Except, it seems, Bank of America's board of directors." Lewis resigned in early October 2009. Brian Moynihan assumed the CEO role in January of 2010 after an eleven-week executive search. Turns out Moynihan rose through the ranks of FleetBoston Financial Corp, which was acquired by Bank of America in 2004.

In 2010, Hewlett Packard's CEO Mark Hurd was succeeded on an interim basis by Catherine Lesjak, the company's executive vice president and chief financial officer. Lesjak was succeeded by Leo Apotheker, who was succeeded eleven months later by Meg Whitman, an HP board member.

These are but two of many examples that suggest not all boards are prepared to deal with the abrupt departures of their CEOs. While these blunders seem unbelievable, especially among large publicly traded companies, the aftermath of similar situations can be devastating to middle-market companies. The business models of the high technology company that lost its CTO demonstrated that in Chapter 1.

Who is watching when the CEO's job becomes vacant? Current and potential investors who could choose to stop investing, customers who could choose to stop buying, employees who lose confidence causing productivity to plummet and turnover to escalate, external candidates who run for the hills, and the news media who launches a frenzy sizeable enough to make executives and board members start wearing hats and dark glasses. That's who.

Associations like the National Association of Corporate Directors and the Corporate Directors Group are resources for board member education and best practices, including information on CEO SPM. They make it crystal clear who is responsible for CEO succession planning. It is unequivocally the responsibility of the board of directors. And if the board hasn't produced a CEO succession plan then it is just a matter of time before investors and other external parties turn up the heat. They want peace of mind knowing the return on their investment does not take a nosedive due to the absence of a contingency plan for CEO departure, planned or not.

What gets in the way of the board taking responsibility for talent management oversight? The study conducted by the Knightsbridge Human Capital Solutions and the Clarkson Centre for Board Effectiveness, in partnership with the Institute of Corporate Directors[1] reported the barriers as:

69% Time constraints, too focused on other issues

65% Lack of resources to prepare themselves to provide talent management oversight

64% Lack of human capital expertise to create the SPM process and guide the board through talent issues

62% CEO and executive team feel threatened when the board gets involved in talent oversight

When should the board begin the CEO succession planning process? As soon as it can. Waiting until the CEO departs is a bad idea since it puts so much at risk for a wide range of stakeholders. Waiting until times of lackluster performance or significant turmoil makes it awkward for the board to raise the issue, awkward for the CEO incumbent who will no doubt feel threatened, and affords little time for turnaround when organizational performance is at stake.[2]

Case and point of a small publicly held company in the laser systems business prior to its acquisition. Joseph Verderber, board member, recalls a time when they had a fairly new CEO in place during the start of a turbulent time in the company's history. With locations in North America and a new acquisition in Europe, the need for strong leadership to guide the ship in a prosperous new direction had never been greater.

Long story short, the CEO was ineffective in moving the organization forward largely due to his spoke-hub communication style. He would speak one-on-one with one person, retreat to his office, and then speak with another. Each person walked away with a different understanding after the one-on-ones. Frustrated at the discovery of the inconsistencies and mounting distrust, each person set out on his or her own path, resulting in a fragmented workforce. The CEO's chosen communication style backfired in unifying company. Rather than augmenting the one-on-ones with multi-directional group communications to reinforce a common understanding and direction, he stuck with an ineffective approach.

The board tried two solutions, each with the goal to retain the CEO, before moving to its last resort. Plan A involved working with the CEO in place to improve his effectiveness. It included creating awareness of limitations with the spoke-hub communication style through board feedback, 360° feedback, followed by executive coaching. Plan A resulted in little to no change in the CEO's behavior; Plan A did not work. At the heart of Plan B was the redistribution of responsibilities, relieving the CEO of some operational duties heavy in employee communication. The duties were re-assigned to the CFO with the goal to eventually move him into the COO role. The board was transparent with both executives in conveying the short and long-term goals and reasons behind the redistribution of responsibilities. While the CFO worked tirelessly to make things work, the solution failed. The board had little recourse but to implement Plan C – replace the CEO with an external candidate.

To what does Joe attribute failure of the initial CEO succession plan? First, the board was overly optimistic about being able to keep the CEO in place. No one, including board members, wanted to fire anyone. Lack of CEO genuine support for the CFO in his new operational role and disarray in the European office contributed heavily to the failure too. The lesson is to make the tough call sooner rather than later – especially when there are signs that the executive has little desire, conviction, or is simply unable to overcome a shortcoming that dramatically impacts performance of the organization.

Insert 10-1:

CEO Successor Performance[2]

The November 2011 article entitled "Succeeding at Succession," in the Harvard Business Review cited some interesting conclusions from an 18 month study of 300 CEO transitions at S&P 500 companies conducted by Spencer Stuart:

- Internal and external CEO candidates overall performed about the same.

- Health of the company was the key factor in the best CEO selections:

  o Internal candidates were the best choice in companies performing well.

  o External candidates were the best choice in companies in turmoil.

- Board members who stepped into the role of CEO outperformed all other internal and external candidates.

- The CEOs with the worst performance were those hired into a company as president or COO 18 months prior to being promoted to CEO.

- Hiring criteria used by many boards to evaluate CEO candidates don't correlate with performance. These criteria included: age, college or graduate school, degrees earned, relocation or commuting needs to take the position, early career employment with blue-chip companies.

When boards do take the reins for CEO succession, how do they go about it? They use the fundamental SPM process outlined in Chapter 2 for identifying mid and long-term potential CEO successors. Add to it an emergency action plan for putting an interim CEO in place in case of vacation, sabbatical, accident, disability, death, or unexpected departure. Succession planning discussions of this type can be especially sensitive with CEO owners of family businesses. So, you will want to start early to work through the many nuances.

The short-term emergency action plan naturally will include the name of the CEO's immediate replacement. The action plan should also have sufficient detail so that the board can seamlessly and quickly transfer the reigns to the replacement CEO. It includes very practical information, such as a list of important contacts and how and when they should connect with each other. It includes board resolution documentation necessary to put the replacement CEO in place as well as templates for communicating the change to employees, customers, supply chain, shareholders, and the press. It is in the best interest of the board to discuss the plan with the CEO and replacement CEO to solidify support and keen insight and suggestions. The emergency action plan gets so specific that it often serves as a checklist to the board when facilitating swift implementation.

Mission critical roles warrant board attention too especially those with no identified successors or blue boxers. These questions must be answered:

- What is the short-term solution should a vacancy occur in this role?

- What is the long-term solution?

- For short and long-term solutions, should the critical role be continued in its current state or is it better addressed through the re-distribution of responsibilities or other solution?

- Related: how easy or difficult is it to develop key capabilities among internal candidates or hire external candidates with key capabilities? How long will each option take?

There are a host of short and long-term remedies such as: accelerate the development of internal candidates, identify an internal interim manager or two to three people who collectively perform the responsibilities (analogous to the CEO emergency short-term action plan), hire external blue boxers with short-term "readiness ratings," distribute responsibilities differently to make it easier to develop or hire for key capabilities, and mix and match these approaches.

In the previous chapter, Wanted: Blue Boxers, setting the goal to hire only external candidates with potential to move into a different role in a short period is important to SPM. It is particularly important for any critical role with no named successor. So, measuring the quality of external new hires becomes increasingly more important given its interplay with SPM. Helpful blue boxer metrics include:

- Output and performance

- Amount of time from date of hire until new hire is fully productive

- Retention rate of the new recruits

As with any organizational investment, measuring and monitoring results for increased understanding on what works, what needs refinement, and the return on investment is expected of boards and executive teams. SPM is no exception.

Think of talent analytics as the key performance indicators for the most important source of competitive advantage – people. The message from studies referenced in Chapter 1 is crystal clear: organizational results suffer when the organization runs without benefit of effective talent management practices. And how can you possibly know if SPM is working without measuring and monitoring it?

Before getting into what should be measured in SPM, it's important to recognize that there is a delicate balance between executing talent management solutions and capturing and analyzing the data resulting from them. When the resources needed to capture, analyze and/or report detract from implementation activities, then things are off kilter. That being said, the automation of talent metrics is an important component to any talent strategy which can pay big dividends in the long run. There are human capital software packages, many of the software as a service variety, for every company size and pocket book. Don't let the lack of automation prevent forward momentum. Pick the most important metrics for your organization and build the capability to measure them.

Start by measuring results over time. Analytics can be instrumental in identifying root causes of problems, trends and trajectories and consist of both lead and lag indicators. What do you measure within the context of SPM? There are several key performance indicators which can be measured at levels such as the (1) organization; (2) function and/or department; and (3) manager and typically include:

- Critical position vacancies filled by internal candidates

- Critical roles with no identified successor; blank blue boxes

- Bench strength – critical roles with at least one internal candidate with a "ready rating" of 18 months or less

- Readiness ratings – indicates the employee is ready to take on the new role within a specified timeframe, typically: "ready now," "ready in one to two years," "two to three years," and "three to five years"

- Competency/skills gap analysis

- Best sources of talent to fill competency/skills gaps

- Engagement and retention rates by key employee groups: SPM participants, top performers, blue boxer new recruits, all others

Assuming things play out and a succession transition occurs between people, how is success best measured? By the outcomes generated by the new successor compared with the expected results. Using outcome oriented measures results in being able to answers to these questions:

- Was the transition of responsibility between executives implemented seamlessly?

- Was organizational performance sustained during the transition?

A 2011 study by the Human Capital Institute and Vistage International[3] reported that one quarter to a third of surveyed organizations measured the effectiveness of leadership initiatives by way of observation rather than using strictly a metric-based approach. For instance, the employees who partook in leadership development were observed for changes in their behavior that:

- Influenced interpersonal relationships

- Influenced decisions and results

- Improved employee engagement scores

Adapt and use the observation method for assessing effectiveness of people succession transitions. If the successor had an initial business problem to solve or change management assignment, another key indicator would be - did he/she solve it? Was the change successful? Use established metrics for assessing the status of organizational performance pre- and post-transition.

Many of the executives interviewed had strong feelings about instilling accountability for effective implementation of SPM among executives and people managers. As a result a growing number of them are tying compensation, a portion of bonus or base salary increase, to the achievement of talent related objectives. For instance the $75M manufacturing company introduced earlier, ties 15% to 20% of managements' bonus to the achievement of employee development objectives. It has been my experience that it requires a couple of cycles before introducing accountability of this type takes hold. Managers may not initially take the objectives seriously until real dollars are awarded or forfeited; usually year 2+ results are significantly improved.

 Footnotes

1. The Knightsbridge Human Capital Solutions and the Clarkson Centre for Board Effectiveness, in partnership with the Institute of Corporate Directors, *Study Beyond the CEO - The role of the Board in ensuring organizations have the talent to thrive*, 2011.

2. James M. Citrin and Dayton Ogden, *Succeeding at Succession*, Harvard Business Review November 2011.

3. Human Capital Institute and Vistage International, *Driving Performance and Business Results with Collaborative Executive Development*, 2011.

HIGHLIGHTS

Board best practices in so far as SPM goes:

- Take responsibility for overseeing short and long-term succession of the CEO, as well as for several layers of mission critical roles in the organization.

- Manage SPM as a process and not a onetime intervention by building SPM into board routines; for instance make the review of SPM and relevant talent analytics a quarterly agenda item.

- For larger boards, establish a committee comprised of a subset of board members and external experts responsible for creating and recommending succession plans for board approval.

- Build in executive accountability for generating desired outcomes and ensure accountability is built in at all levels of the organization.

Chapter 11
Ready, Set, Go

Someone in a mission critical role gives notice, has taken ill, or worse, the person dies. Perhaps an executive planning to retire would like to wind down sooner than planned or move out of her current role and into a part-time one as part of winding down. Regardless of the reason for job vacancy, now you must think through the nuances of activating the succession plan before actually putting it in motion.

Why do you need to think the transition through again? Because of the dynamic world in which we live. Internal, external, and situational factors and assumptions made when creating the succession plan may have changed. Plus, during the process you may have identified several options for ensuring a critical job vacancy is filled. Now you must decide which option best serves the organization at this point in time (another form of risk management).

You crafted the succession plan with input from other members of the executive team. When contemplating rollout you'll want to benefit again from the insight of the same executives. After all, the transition may impact them, their responsibilities, and their employees. By confidentially consulting and collaborating with them before settling on the best option they will be more likely to support you, the successor, and everyone else impacted.

When acting on the plan, the successor not only takes on a new role but vacates his/her current role. And that may result in the "domino effect," or a series of role changes/career growth opportunities for several people. Putting all the changes into motion smoothly and seamlessly takes foresight and finesse. This is yet another reason to confidentially engage the other executives.

Why do I stress confidential consultation? Because things can change midstream. And once the cat is out of the bag and (heaven forbid) must be retracted, well, your job unnecessarily got tougher. Keeping conversations limited to those who have a need to know before implementing the change is a first step toward success.

Thinking through for yourself and engaging the other executives in the thinking process has basically three phases: ready, set, and go.

Ready

In the "ready" phase, a number of things are considered before making a decision among the options presented in the succession plan. First, get reacquainted with the potential successors for filling the critical job vacancy. Second, review the assumptions made with each. Third, inventory what will change or has changed since the options were created such as: economic conditions, competitive threats, situational factors, organizational performance as a whole, and performance by segments within the organization. As for segments within the organization, identify those most and least stressed. For those most stressed what capabilities are in greatest demand to turn things around? Are there other pending job vacancies that should be considered in parallel? Fourth, answer these questions for each potential successor:

- Does the potential successor still desire this type of career growth?

- Is the potential successor ready for the new assignment? If not entirely, what else needs to happen in order to make the transition a success?

- What impact will removing the potential successor from his/her current organization have on its performance and employees?

- What impact will the potential successor have on the new organization, its performance, and employees?

- How will you know if the successor is successful?

Fifth, evaluate the options and decide which one will be implemented because it makes the most sense for the organization. Sixth, identify the potential successors not selected for new role, associated flight risks, and new career growth opportunities moving forward, if any.

Case and point: Jonathan Burke, Vice President of Visitor Services and Operations at MOS, recalls when he had a job opening due to expansion of his division. Jonathan needed someone to oversee either the customer service or the operations part of the division. He did not feel compelled to explore external candidates given a couple of internal candidates, let's call them Joe and Maggie, each with their own talents and career growth aspirations.

Jonathan got to know the candidates largely by way of cross-functional projects. Moving Joe into the position, given his considerable strengths and expertise, would have resulted in his oversight of divisional operations. Moving Maggie would have resulted in her leading customer service and sales. Embedded in the decision was who might succeed Jonathan in the future if he were to leave MOS. Jonathan decided providing oversight to customer service was the way to go. Maggie was a very strong performer, had a track record for producing great results, and the skill set required to manage customer service. This choice played to Maggie's strengths and Maggie did not disappoint demonstrated by her achievement of record breaking membership sales growth in subsequent years. This success was made, in large part, due to Maggie's oversight of the program as well as the sales outlets which were embedded in the division.

Set

The "set" stage involves putting together an implementation schedule for the option selected. At a minimum it includes: the timing of personnel changes with specifics on the roles and responsibilities assigned to each person, knowledge transfer specifics, and temporary work arrangements and their duration, if any.

Once the foundation for the implementation schedule is crafted then go back and insert important action items as well as who's responsible for completing them. Include conversations with affected people. Some people will be directly affected, those whose roles have changed for instance. For this group you will want to have finite details on things like their new goals, expectations, support, direct reports, titles, and compensation changes, if any. Plus you will want to assign them the task of preparing their own "on-boarding" plan for their new role and working with you to shape the transition.

Subsequent action items include communicating the change to groups of people affected such as those who will gain or lose a leader. This may involve the preparation of verbal and/or written announcements of organizational changes made to stakeholders at large followed by small group meetings.

Don't overlook circling back with potential successors not chosen for the new role as they are sure to feel disappointed, overlooked, and underappreciated. This is best completed the same day as the formal announcements. Let them know the decision, reinforce their value to the organization, and commit to re-connecting soon to discuss other career growth opportunities. Then follow through!

Take one last pass on the implementation schedule and make sure it is not too tight and does not drag out for too long. If the schedule is too tight, then important insights gathered via employee conversations get lost in the shuffle. This can result in alienating employees or paving the way for a bumpy implementation. Running too long does nothing more than fuel the rumor mill; people are very good at sensing when something is up. Employees in the know may share snippets of information confidentially with trusted colleagues. And employees often get creative in filling in the remaining gaps in the absence of accurate information.

Go

The "go" stage starts with executing the implementation schedule. As stated earlier, insights and recommendations collected in the employee conversations may influence future steps.

The manager will want to set aside time to jointly create a concrete "on-boarding plan" with the successor. On-boarding plans, initially designed for use by new external hires, are just as valuable to internal hires too. On-boarding is especially important for employees who move to other parts of the organization where their personal networks are sparse. And development doesn't stop when an employee takes on the new role; rather, it's continued and reflected in the on-boarding plan. The on-boarding plan will articulate expected results and a road map for achieving them. Plus it will encompass check-ins between successor and his/her manager to provide feedback, monitor progress on achievement of personal and organizational goals, and formulate and refine strategies for future challenges.

The manager will also want to informally check-in with employees affected by the leadership changes just to assess if things are on track. This is often accomplished using informal and formal means. The sooner the successor gets solid feedback, the sooner adjustments can be made to gain or regain momentum.

Case and point: When Ken Margossian was a division executive of a large company, he was selected to succeed the president. He and the president worked out a transition plan to transpire over the course of four to five months; the collective thinking behind the plan was valuable. As it turned out, however, Ken was handed the keys to the corner office and a list of charitable donation commitments made by his predecessor about two days after his promotion was announced. Ken's predecessor unexpectedly headed off to a new assignment as president of the parent holding company, which was in crisis. While the transition plan largely flew out the window, Ken carried on very successfully. Ken's initial takeaway, first heard from a mentor early in his career, was that it's often easier to hire strong functional experts then to hire strong leaders. There are times when strong leaders are needed in a hurry. And his second takeaway was the value of thinking through a transition despite the fact Ken had to go it alone when it came to execution.

HIGHLIGHTS

- Refer to the succession plan when a job vacancy occurs; that's what it's there for.

- Confidentially consult with the executive team members who collectively put the plan together; after all, a newly named successor will impact them, their teams and areas of responsibility.

- Consider all internal candidate options taking into account their capabilities as well as internal, external, and situational factors, and assumptions that may have changed since the plan was put together.

- Once a deployment decision is made, create a transition plan with the successor.

- Ensure the successor gets quality feedback often and acts on it to maximize effectiveness.

Afterthoughts

Most organizations don't decide to "make *or* buy," when it comes to talent. Rather, their decision-making focuses on the right mix of "make *and* buy" to fill talent gaps. There's no denying the strong interdependency between hiring internal candidates via SPM and external candidates via recruiting programs.

Recruiting programs designed to hire external candidates may need to be revamped. Starting with some recruiting analytics, targeted recruiting (even if it takes you abroad) will become increasingly more prevalent as will generational specific recruiting approaches.

Other people practices may warrant change too. For instance, organizations will need to redesign their retirement practices to entice employees nearing retirement to stay longer in full or part-time capacities. Organizations may need to overhaul flexible work arrangements to address changes in family structure and the growing number of women in the workforce, if they haven't already. And deliberate initiatives to help long-service employees maintain their competitive edge for fueling innovation will warrant future investment.

Figure 12-1: Succession Planning & Management Process

SPM Cycle Complete

A successor taking on the role that he or she's been preparing for might seem like the end game of SPM (Figure 12-1). Untrue. The SPM cycle continues. There are triggers that may prompt changes in SPM. For instance, when the business strategy changes resulting in the demand for different mission critical capabilities, then SPM should change too. Should unwanted turnover skyrocket then adjustments for enriching and advancing career progression will ensue. And when demographics in the workforce at large shift then so will the balance of external and internal candidate hiring. These are but a few reasons for embracing SPM into your company's culture.

Why else does SPM make sense for your organization? Because:

- Mission critical roles are filled quickly and cost effectively from a qualified talent pool comprised of internal employees.

- SPM reduces the risk of business disruptions and organizational underperformance due to job vacancies or key roles held by people not fully prepared.

- SPM improves engagement and retention rates among participating employees.

- SPM addresses workforce challenges posed by shifting demographics.

- Recruiting external candidates alone will not satisfy your current and future talent needs.

Why should you personally bother with SPM? Because you:

- Have an unwavering desire to position your organization for growth.

- Choose to manage risk, all major risks, that could compromise company growth.

- Possess a deeply seeded belief that proactive talent management is your duty.

- Intend to tackle the complex challenge posed by future skills and talent shortages.

- Promote a talent management journey where solutions are practical, adaptable, sustainable and tightly linked to business strategy.

- Are driven to help others succeed!

When I set out to write this peer learning in print publication I had two objectives. My first objective was that by the time you finished reading this book you could imagine what it would be like to have many more options when it comes to assembling and redeploying a robust, adaptable, and high performance workforce. The myriad of remarkable experiences and results shared in this publication accomplished this objective and more.

My second objective was that you decide to make SPM a priority and enlist others in your organization to build an internal talent pool as a risk management imperative. SPM is a type of insurance policy for one of the largest and most important investments your organization will make – human capital. Accomplishing this second objective is entirely up to you!

About the Author

Carol Bergeron is a consultant, coach, facilitator, speaker, author, and the President of Bergeron Associates™. She launched the firm in 1998 after more than 15 years in senior leadership corporate positions with a focus on human capital management. Today, Bergeron Associates™ helps clients achieve their goals by transforming leaders into powerful talent magnets who get business results.

Noted specialties of Carol's firm include leadership development, succession planning & talent management, workforce planning & integration, and workforce capability building through consulting, training, speaking and coaching services.

In addition to her consulting work, Carol has facilitated leadership sessions at the Boston University Corporate Education Center and Bentley University. She has spoken at the CEO Resources Forum, The Executive Committee, Mass Bio Tech Council, International Society

Pharmaceutical Engineers, Society for Information Management Systems, WPI Venture Forum, Medical Development Group, Organizational Development Learning Group, Institute of Management Consultants, and numerous Human Resources Associations.

Recipient of the "Best of 2008" Award in the CEO Refresher, Carol has been published in the Handbook of Business Strategy, Leadership Excellence, NonProfit World, Womens' Business Boston, IndUS Business Journal, and Society for Human Resource Management. She publishes a popular monthly newsletter blog: www.bergeronassociates.com/blog.

Carol is an active member of several organizations including the Association for Corporate Growth, Healthcare Business Women's Association, and Human Resources Leadership Forum, and is past President of the Institute of Management Consultants of New England. Carol earned a B.S. in Business Administration from the University of Vermont and can best be reached by visiting her website at www.bergeronassociates.com.

Bonus Content

To access bonus content made available exclusively to you follow these two easy steps.

1. Go to:

   www.bergeronassociates.com/135357content and create an account.

   Your contact information is stored confidentially and will not be shared with anyone outside of Bergeron Associates™.

2. When your account has been activated then you will receive notification with a link to access the bonus content.

Please feel free to login into your account from time to time to access fresh new bonus content on people succession and related topics.